EZRA POUND AND JAPANESE NOH PLAYS

Nobuko Tsukui

UNIVERSITY
PRESS OF
AMERICA

Copyright © 1983 by
University Press of America, Inc.™
P.O. Box 19101, Washington, D.C. 20036

All rights reserved

Printed in the United States of America

Library of Congress Cataloging in Publication Data

Tsukui, Nobuko.
  Ezra Pound and Japanese noh plays.

  Bibliography: p.
  Includes index.
  1. Nō plays--Translations into English--History and criticism. 2. American drama--Translations from Japanese--History and criticism. 3. Pound, Ezra, 1885-1972--Knowledge--Language and languages. 4. Pound, Ezra, 1885-1972--Knowledge--Performing arts. 5. Pound, Ezra, 1885-1972--Friends and associates. 6. Fenollasa, Ernest Francisco, 1853-1908. I. Title.
  PL735.T77 1983   895.6'2'009   82-23833
  ISBN 0-8191-2987-9
  ISBN 0-8191-2988-7 (pbk.)

To

Paul A. Olson

ACKNOWLEDGEMENTS

Quotation from John Hamilton Edwards, et al., Annotated Index to the Cantos of Ezra Pound. Copyright © 1957 by the Regents of the University of California. Reprinted by permission of the University of California Press.

Quotations from Ernest F. Fenollosa, Epochs of Chinese and Japanese Art: An Outline History of East Asiatic Design. Vol. I. New and revised edition with copious notes by Professor Petrucci, 1963. Reprinted by permission of Dover Publications, Inc.

Quotation from Earl Miner, The Japanese Tradition in British and American Literature. Copyright © 1958 by Princeton University Press. Reprinted by permission of Princeton University Press.

Quotation from Ezra Pound, Make It New: Essays by Ezra Pound. Copyright 1935 by Yale University Press. Reprinted by permission of Yale University Press.

Quotation from Noel Stock, ed., Ezra Pound: Perspectives. 1965. This book is out of print and no longer available. Reprinted by permission of Contemporary Books, Inc.

Quotation from Noel Stock, Poet in Exile: Ezra Pound. Copyright 1964 by Barnes & Noble Books. Reprinted by permission of Barnes & Noble Books, Totowa, New Jersey.

Quotations from Roy E. Teele, "A Balance Sheet on Pound's Translations of Noh Plays," Books Abroad, Vol. 39, published by the University of Oklahoma Press. Copyright 1965 by the University of Oklahoma Press. Reprinted by permission of the University of Oklahoma Press.

Quotations from The No Plays of Japan. Translated from the Japanese by Arthur Waley. Copyright © under the Berne Convention. All rights reserved. Reprinted by permission of Grove Press, Inc.

Excerpts from all of the following:

    Ezra Pound, ABC of Reading. Copyright 1934 by Ezra Pound.

v

Ezra Pound, Guide to Kulchur. All Rights Reserved.

Ezra Pound, Selected Letters of Ezra Pound 1907-1941. Copyright 1950 by Ezra Pound.

Ezra Pound, The Cantos of Ezra Pound. Copyright 1934, 1937, 1940, 1948 by Ezra Pound. Copyright © 1956, 1959, 1962, 1965, 1968, 1970 by Ezra Pound.

Ezra Pound, The Classic Noh Theatre of Japan. Copyright © 1959 by New Directions Publishing Corporation.

Ezra Pound, Yoro. Copyright © 1975 by the Trustees of the Ezra Pound Library Property Trust.

All of the above reprinted by permission of New Directions Publishing Corporation.

The first chapter of this book is based on the essay which first appeared in The Markham Review and is reproduced with revisions by permission of the editor.

The second chapter is an extensive revision of two articles which appeared in Literature East & West and in Paideuma.

CONTENTS

Page

INTRODUCTION ix

CHAPTER I POUND'S RELATIONSHIP WITH

    FENOLLOSA AND NOH PLAYS

    (1) Notes on the Noh Play 1

    (2) Pound's Relationship with

        Fenollosa and Noh Plays 7

CHAPTER II EZRA POUND'S VERSION OF THE NOH PLAYS

    (1) Introduction 31

    (2) Sotoba Komachi 33

    (3) Nishikigi 40

    (4) Aoi no Ue 46

    (5) Kinuta 54

CHAPTER III EZRA POUND'S TRANSLATIONS OF

    ELEVEN MORE NOH PLAYS 67

APPENDIX I 95

APPENDIX II 97

BIBLIOGRAPHY 113

INDEX 117

INTRODUCTION

Despite considerable linguistic deficiencies, Ezra Pound accepted the task of completing the English translation of the Japanese Noh plays left unfinished by Ernest Fenollosa (1853-1908), an American scholar educated at Harvard, who spent a number of years in Japan, and became an authority on Japanese arts and literature. Noh is a form of drama, written partly in prose and partly in verse, dating from the late fourteenth century and consisting of singing, dialogue and dancing, with the use of masks and a symbolic stage as its most unique characteristics.[1] Since the publication of the English translation of the fifteen Noh plays in 1917, critics--including Pound himself--have expressed dissatisfaction with the work, pointing out such flaws as misunderstandings, inaccuracies and distortions.[2] The primary purpose of this study is to investigate the nature and the quality of Pound's translations and the kinds of problems they present, and to suggest how we may approach Pound's work.

By close examination of a few representative plays translated by Pound, I have attempted to answer these questions: (1) If Pound misunderstood Noh, what aspects of it did he fail to understand--plot, subject matter, stage convention, style, characterization, or religious significance? (2) If his translations are inaccurate, are all the fifteen plays equally inadequate? Or, does the degree of inaccuracy vary from play to play? If the distortion or deviation exists in Pound's translations, what part of a play did he change and in what way? How does the deviation affect the play?

The study of the plays translated by Pound shows that the problems differ depending on the individual plays. For example, in his translation of Sotoba Komachi and Tamura, Pound leaves out great portions of the original text, whereas in translating Nishikigi, Kinuta and Hagoromo, he sometimes adds words, phrases or lines to the original. For my study I chose the four plays--Sotoba Komachi, Kinuta, Nishikigi and Aoi no Ue--which best represent the most essential qualities of Pound's translations--both in their merits and demerits.

In Chapter I the focus is on three major topics: (1) the explanatory comments on the Noh plays; (2) Ezra Pound's relationship with Ernest Fenollosa--how Pound came to assume the responsibility of Fenollosa's literary executor; and (3) the significance of the Noh plays in Pound's literary career--how he used Noh in his other works, both prose and poetry.

Chapter II makes a detailed study of each of the four plays in comparison with their Japanese originals. After the extensive discussion of the four individual plays in the second chapter, Chapter III deals with the remaining eleven plays translated by Pound. In this chapter, the review centers on Pound's version of each play in relation to the rest of the plays, focusing on the most significant aspects, rather than analyzing the whole, of the play. This chapter will show several basic characteristics of Pound's translations.

It is hoped that the present study will throw a certain light on Ezra Pound's translations of the Noh plays and will enable the reader to gain a clearer insight into the quality of the work under discussion, even if he does not have the necessary language proficiency to understand Pound's translations in reference to the original texts.

Notes to Introduction

1. See Ch. I, the notes on the Noh plays, for a further explanation on Noh.

2. For Pound's comment on his own work, see Ch. I. Professor Earl Miner writes: "The Pound-Fenollosa version is a poet's translation. Scholarly where he can be, but unfamiliar with the historical, literary, and linguistic contexts, Pound undertook an impossible task in his translation. As often as not he has succeeded, and where he has his translations are not infrequently superior to Waley's in quality. But he often fails. He botches the end of Kinuta so that it makes little sense and unaccountably cuts Sotoba Komachi down to an insignificant two pages, where Waley uses eleven. Some faults must be ascribed to Fenollosa or to the imperfect state of his notes, but there is no excuse for the introduction to Awoi no Uye [also spelled "Aoi no Ue"] which muddles a fine translation. Also, considering his great poetic powers, Hagoromo is a disappointment, perhaps the greatest of all. He understood the play perfectly, translated much of it superbly, and yet the end of the play, one of the most beautiful passages in no [sic], is put into a prose which bumps along heavily at the end." (Earl Miner, The Japanese Tradition in British and American Literature [Princeton, New Jersey: Princeton University Press, 1958], p. 137) In regard to Pound's handling of the religious elements in the Noh plays, Professor Roy E. Teele says: ". . . Pound did not study Buddhism and Shintoism. . . thoroughly, but instead slipped into errors through following the snare of superficial resemblances between these religious elements and 'western' spiritualism and even Irish folklore. . ." (Roy E. Teele, "A Balance Sheet on Pound's Translations of Noh Plays," Books Abroad [Spring 1965], Vol. 39, p. 169.) See also Ch. II for further comments on Aoi no Ue by Arthur Waley.

CHAPTER I

POUND'S RELATIONSHIP

WITH FENOLLOSA AND NOH PLAYS

(1) Notes on the Noh Play

Noh was developed from sarugaku, a performing art consisting of singing, dialogue and dancing. The most significant event in the history of the Noh play took place in 1374, when the performance of Kan'ami and his son Zeami[1] at Jinji Sarugaku (the Sarugaku performance dedicated to the Shinto shrine) in Kyoto won the recognition of Shogun Ashikaga Yoshimitsu. From then on, under the patronage of the Shogun, and partly due to the efforts of the Noh masters, this performing art improved its artistic quality and, during the lifetime of Zeami, established itself as a unique yet highly artistic form of drama. There are at least 2,000 Noh plays extant, of which about 240 are played today. Of these 240 plays about 100 are attributed to Zeami. Of the fifteen plays translated by Ezra Pound, Suma Genji, Nishikigi, Kinuta, Kakitsubata and Aoi no Ue (there is some dispute over the authorship of the last play) were written by Zeami. From the beginning Noh had a close relationship to both Buddhism and Shintoism, the two dominant religions in Japan. More than half of the 240 plays are religiously motivated.

Dancing and music are important elements of Noh. As Arthur Waley, whose book, The No Plays of Japan, is the first authoritative English translation of Noh, explains: "At its simplest, the Noh play consists of a dance preceded by a dialogue which explains the significance of the dance or introduces circumstances which lead naturally to the dancing of it."[2] In a Noh play specific terms are given to the characters. "Shite" is the chief character--hero or heroines. That is, Shite can be either male or female. Shite is the dancer and the doer of a play. "Waki" is the subordinate character; he is to explain the situation and usually does not participate in the action of the play; sometimes, there are two "Waki" in a play. "Tsure" is an adjunct or companion, who can be a companion of either "Shite" or "Waki"; thus, there can be more than one "Tsure" in a play. Also there is the chorus, consisting of ten to twelve men. In the Noh play, all the actors are men. As for music, only four musical instruments are used: <u>fue</u> (a flute); <u>kotsuzumi</u> (a small hand-drum); <u>otsuzumi</u> (a large hand-drum); and <u>taiko</u> (a stick-drum; not always used). Because of the extremely limited number of the instruments, the music played in a Noh play is necessarily simple in tone. Although music is a very important element in Noh, it does not have an independent significance, but serves as a background.

The use of masks is one unique characteristic of Noh. As a general rule, Shite always wears a mask (with only a few exceptions). Since all the Noh actors are men, all the female characters--regardless of whether they are Shite, Waki, or Tsure--wear masks. For the rest of the characters (male Waki and male Tsure), their nature, or what they are (man, god, or supernatural being), and their age determine whether or not they wear masks. Perhaps the masks for female characters are the most highly developed, and those for old men come next. There are varieties of masks for women of different ages, ranks and personalities. The experts of Noh often point out a kind of paradox in the Noh mask: though a mask is static, it can express, not just one, but different shades of the feelings of the wearer, if it is made by a skilled artist. In general, the Noh costume may be characterized as colorful and luxurious. The costume of female characters is especially elaborate.

In contrast to the costumes, the Noh stage, which is extremely simple, gives an impression of bareness. No curtain is used. Stage-sets are more symbolic than realistic. They greatly rely on the imagination of the audience. There are only a few stage properties. Of these a fan is the most important. It is said that no actor appears on the stage without a fan somewhere on his person. A fan in a Noh play represents many things--a sword, a wine-cup, a knife, a saw, a mallet.

Noh plays may be divided into two major categories: <u>mugen-noh</u> (Noh plays of dreams and phantasms) and <u>genzai-noh</u> (Noh plays of the real world). The first kind, <u>mugen-noh</u>, may be described as follows: A traveller comes to a famous place. Then an inhabitant of the place or a villager arrives. The villager tells the traveller a legend pertaining to the place. At the end of his tale, the villager disappears, saying that he is really the character so-and-so in the story just told. The disappearance of the villager, who is usually the Shite, is called nakairi (a recess in the middle), meaning the principal actor's temporary exit. While the traveller is waiting, the villager reappears, this time, in the form of the character described in the previous tale. The Shite (the Shite in disguise in the first part of the play is called the First Shite, and the Shite in his true form after nakairi is called the Second Shite) in his true form tells the traveller a story of his past life, or dances for the traveller. Finally at dawn he disappears. (At this point it is often the case that the traveller awakes from his sleep and finds that everything took place in his dream.) The Shite can be a famous beauty, a noble prince, or a dead man tortured in the Buddhist "Purgatory". Sometimes the Shite is a god, a devil, or the spirit of some flower. Also the traveller, who is usually the Waki, can be either male or female; he can be a priest, a courtier, or something else. But, quite often the Waki is a travelling priest. The plot of the mugen-noh is in most cases uniform. The highlight of the mugen-noh is the tale and dance of the Shite in both forms. The traveller, or the Waki, on the other hand, is used only to introduce the Shite and to explain the situation at the beginning; and after he finishes his part, he sits at the edge of the stage and watches the acting of the Shite. Thus, in a mugen-noh play, the main part of the play is acted by the Shite, or the chief character, alone. Its subject matter varies, but its form does not—the mugen-noh takes the form of a reminiscence of the Shite.

The second type, called the genzai-noh, presents the world of actuality. And it does not have such a striking uniformity as the mugen-noh has. From the description of the mugen-noh it may be obvious that many Noh plays are divided into two parts. And some genzai-noh plays are also divided into two parts. Of the fifteen plays translated by Pound, Sotoba Komachi, Kinuta and Kagekiyo belong to the genzai-noh group; Kayoi Komachi, Aoi no Ue, Kumasaka, Suma Genji, Tamura, Nishikigi, Tsunemasa, Genjo and Choryo belong to the mugen-noh. Hagoromo, Kakitsubata and Shojo are the mixture of both elements.

There is another and, perhaps, more widely known classification of the Noh plays, according to which the plays are divided into five groups: (1) a god-play, or a play of prayer in which the chief character is a god; (2) a battle-play in which the chief character is a warrior who, in most plays, is tortured in the Buddhist "Purgatory" after death; (3) a "wig"-play, or a female-play in which the chief character is a woman, who wears a wig--hence, a "wig" play; (4) a play of "madness" in which the chief character is a mad woman; however, this group includes various types of plays which do not belong to any of the other four groups; and (5) a "demon"-play in which the chief character is often a supernatural being, either friendly or hostile to human beings. Of the 240 plays which are performed today, thirty-nine belong to the first group; sixteen to the second; thirty-eight to the third; ninety-four to the fourth; and fifty-three to the fifth.³

By the seventeenth century, the order of plays to be performed in one day had become fixed. Ordinarily five plays (one from each of the five groups) were presented in the order described above. That is to say, the day of Noh performance began with a god-play and ended with a demon-play. Today, however, it is seldom that all five plays are performed on the same day, chiefly because it is impractical to have the audience sit in a Noh theatre for so many hours. Of the fifteen plays translated by Pound, none belongs to the first group, the god-play; Tamura and Tsunemasa belong to the second, the battle-play; Kakitsubata and Hagoromo belong to the third, the "wig"-play; Sotoba Komachi, Kayoi Komachi, Kinuta, Nishikigi, Aoi no Ue and Kagekiyo belong to the fourth group; Kumasaka, Choryo, Genjo and Shojo belong to the fifth group. Suma Genji is sometimes included in the fourth and sometimes in the fifth group.

The fact that the Noh plays can be divided into five groups indicates that the range of subject matters in Noh is not very great. Furthermore, not every Noh play has a definite subject matter or a definable central idea. For example, in Shojo, the main interest of the play is in its music and dancing, and the story or ideas are secondary. And in the first half of Sotoba Komachi the play on words, under the guise of a religious disputation, is the main interest. But many plays do have some definable subject matters. Often they concern the grace of the gods, love, jealousy, the heroism of a great warrior and the agony of his ghost, or the nobility of a great prince. Whether a play has a subject matter or not depends on its author: some authors seem to have written plays without paying much attention to themes or ideas, emphasizing rather other aspects, such as dancing, music or the play on words and sophistry.

    The Noh plays are written partly in prose and partly in verse. Two styles are used in prose portions: one is the so-called <u>soro</u> style, in which an auxiliary verb <u>soro</u>[4] is added to each main verb. This style is most commonly found in the dialogue of a Noh play. The other is the style in which the auxiliary <u>soro</u> is not used. This second style is less often used in the prose portions, for it is the style in which all the verse portions are written. The <u>soro</u> style is more conversational and less refined than the other style, which may be called the verse style. Therefore, the <u>soro</u> style is used for the speech of the characters of lower classes. On the other hand the verse style is used for the speech of the characters of high rank and prestige. The verse style, because it is compact, is also capable of conveying the tension and strain of the situation, or the emotion, much better than the <u>soro</u> style, which is more relaxed. Thus, when the situation becomes tense, even the speech of a low character changes from the <u>soro</u> to the verse style.

    As there are two styles used in the prose portions, so there are two kinds of verse used in verse portions. One may be called prose verse. In this first kind, no formal or distinguishable rhythmical pattern exists. The other kind has a distinct rhythmical pattern, though of course it allows variations. The dominant rhythmical pattern is the repetition of alternate lines of seven and five syllables. In the verse portions the play on the words, especially the employment of puns on place names and personal names, is frequent.

    We may, then, raise a question: how do we distinguish between the non-<u>soro</u> prose and the prose verse? Sometimes we can distinguish between the two, based on several criteria: whether or not a certain passage uses puns and other rhetorical devices--if it uses such devices, it is considered verse. Or, non-<u>soro</u> prose is used often in the earlier part of a play, but seldom in the middle or latter part, whereas prose verse may be used throughout. Occasionally, playwrights explicitly indicate that a certain part is meant to be "prose narrative." However, these are vague criteria and subject to many exceptions. The truth is that it is often extremely difficult to tell the difference between the "prose," the contents of which are highly emotional and strained, and the "verse" without definite rhythmical patterns. Therefore, for my study, unless there is a clear indication in the original text that a certain part is "prose," I consider only those parts which are written in the <u>soro</u> style as "prose," and the rest--both prose verse <u>and</u> verse with distinct rhythmical patterns--as "verse." In translating the Noh plays into English, both Waley and Pound distinguish between prose and verse, but neither makes any further distinction.[5]

One final remark should be made. The Noh plays often use existing literary materials. For example, <u>Suma Genji</u> and <u>Aoi no Ue</u> are based on the <u>Tale of Genji</u> by Lady Murasaki (978-1016?), and <u>Kakitsubata</u> is partly based on <u>Ise Monogatari</u>.[6] There are numerous quotations from the Buddhist scriptures and other literary materials.

(2) Pound's Relationship with Fenollosa and Noh Plays

'Noh' or Accomplishment: A Study of the Classical Stage of Japan was published in 1917 under the authorship of Ernest Fenollosa and Ezra Pound. Ernest Fenollosa, born in Salem, Massachusetts, in 1853 and educated at Harvard, went to Japan at the age of twenty-five as a "Professor of Political Economy and Philosophy" at the University of Tokyo. Mrs. Fenollosa writes: "From 1878 until 1886 he was, every recurrent two years, re-appointed to his Chair in the University. 'Professor of Logic,' and, later on, 'Professor of Aesthetics,' were added to his official titles. From the first year he had become deeply interested in an art new to him, the art of Old Japan, and, it must be added, of Old China, too, for in Japan the one cannot be studied without the other."[8] Fenollosa himself writes: "In Boston I had studied Art as a philosopher, and had also attempted the practice of it. Here, in Japan, I became regarded as an antiquarian, an authority, and before many years was appointed a Japanese commissioner for research, administration, and Art education."[9]

Fenollosa's acquaintance with the Noh plays seems to have begun in 1882. Mrs. Fenollosa writes: "In this same year [1882] a minor study, of which something must be said later on, was taken up. This was of the sacred drama called 'No,' sometimes spelled in France and England 'Noh.' He found in it most interesting analogies with early morality plays of Europe, and especially with earliest forms of Greek drama. His teacher was Umewaka Minoru, who, before the great break-up [the Meiji Restoration] of 1868, was court actor to the Shogun."[10] During his stay in Japan, Fenollosa studied the Noh plays with considerable enthusiasm and apparently translated a number of the plays into English. Fenollosa, however, did not find an opportunity to work out his rough translations which are said to be written in pencil, before he died suddenly in 1908 in London. Thus, his unfinished translations together with his other literary remains were left with his widow, who, after several years' search, found in Pound the qualifications for her husband's literary executor.[11] According to Pound, "it was at Sarojini Naidu's[12] that I met Fenollosa's widow through whom

7

came my first contact with the great poetry of Japan and China. . ."[13] Pound's meeting with Mrs. Fenollosa appears to have taken place in 1913. This conjecture is based on the fact that Pound never mentioned the Fenollosa manuscripts in any of his published works or letters prior to December, 1913, when for the first time we see him mention "Fenollosa's treasures in mss." in his letter to William Carlos Williams: "I am very placid and happy and busy. Dorothy is learning Chinese. I've all old Fenollosa's treasurers in mss."[14] Pound's letter to Louis Untermeyer, written shortly after this one, tells a little more about "Fenollosa's treasures": "I've come in for Fenollosa's very valuable mss. on the Japanese 'Noh' plays & the Chinese Lyric. I suppose I'll have the first paper on same in the 'Quarterly Review' for about May" (8 January, 1914).[15] According to Noel Stock, "The papers which Mrs Fenollosa gave to Pound included an unfinished manuscript of the essay on 'The Chinese Written Character as a Medium for Poetry', literal rough translations of a number of Noh plays into English, together with notes about the Noh, which Pound first published in book form in 1916. . ., and a series of notebooks containing notes which Fenollosa made while studying ancient Chinese literature under Professor Mori. . ."[16] Some of the materials listed here are now housed in the Ezra Pound Archives[17] at Beinecke Library of Yale University, including the drafts--"literal rough translations"--of ten out of the fifteen Noh plays which were eventually printed in the Noh. A thorough examination of these drafts vis-à-vis the final, printed versions will be an interesting and probably rewarding project to pursue. Here, however, let it suffice to note that the conditions of these "Fenollosa manuscripts" vary considerably,[18] that it is not certain how much more material on Noh was contained in the very original Fenollosa manuscripts, and that, consequently, some of the questions raised in the present study concerning the state of the real original Fenollosa manuscripts as they were handed to Pound might remain unanswered even after these materials at Beinecke Library have been carefully examined.

At any rate, Pound seems to have started to work on the Noh plays in the Fenollosa manuscripts soon after he received them. His letter to Harriet Monroe in January, 1914 concerns itself with the Noh plays and is important in that it shows Pound's high estimate for the aesthetics of the form. It is worth quoting in its entirety:

> Dear H.M.: Here is the Japanese play for April. [Nishikigi] It will give us some reason for existing. I send it in place of my own stuff, as my name is in such opprobrium we will not mention who did the extracting. Anyhow Fenollosa's name is enough.
>
> These plays are in Japanese, part in verse, part in prose. Also I have written the stuff as prose where the feet are rather uniform. It will save space and keep the thing from filling too much of the number.
>
> There's a long article with another play to appear in The Quarterly. This Nishikigi is too beautiful to be encumbered with notes and long explanation. Besides I think it is now quite lucid—my landlady and grocer both say the story is clear anyhow. Fenollosa, as you probably know, is dead. I happen to be acting as literary executor, but no one need know that yet awhile.
>
> I think you will agree with me that this Japanese find is about the best bit of luck we've had since the starting of the magazine [Poetry]. I don't put the work under the general category of translation either. It could scarcely have come before now. The earlier attempts to do Japanese in English are dull and ludicrous. That you needn't mention either as the poor scholars have done their bungling best. One can not commend the results. The best plan is to say nothing about it. This present stuff ranks as recreation. You'll find W.B.Y. also very keen on it. (Letters, # 36. London, 31 January, 1914).

In another letter to Harriet Monroe in March, 1914 Pound writes: "No, the Fenollosa play can't wait. It won't do any harm to print it with the Yeats stuff in May. Every number ought to be at least as 'sublimated' as such a number will be. If we can't stay that good we ought to quit" (Letters, # 42. London, 28 March, 1914). His work on the Fenollosa manuscripts continued as he writes to Amy Lowell in April, 1914: "I am on my head with Fenollosa notes and the expectable disturbances of such a season" (Letters, # 44. Coleman's Hatch, 30 April, 1914).[19] Finally, in 1916 Certain Noble Plays of Japan with W. B. Yeats' introduction was published by the Cuala Press (Dublin, Ireland).[20] In 1917 the same text was published in the U. S. by Alfred A. Knopf, Inc. as 'Noh' or Accomplishment: A Study of the Classical Stage of Japan.[21]

In the "Note" to Noh Pound summarizes his role in the book as follows: "The vision and the plan are Fenollosa's. In the prose I have had but the part of literary executor; in the plays my work has been that of translator who has found all the heavy work done for him and who has but the pleasure of arranging beauty into the words" (Noh, "Note"). It is obvious, from the foregoing discussion, that Noh is the work started by Fenollosa and completed by Pound. To be more accurate, however, the book is actually the work of three men, as Professor Teele explains: "Hirata Kiichi, a Japanese student who helped Ernest Fenollosa by preparing rough versions of plays he and Mrs. Fenollosa were about to see performed; Fenollosa himself, who apparently not only revised Hirata's work but also translated arias he was learning to sing; and Ezra Pound. . ."[22] In the same "Note," a part of which was quoted above, Pound writes: "I wish to express my very deep thanks to Mr. Arthur Waley, who has corrected a number of mistakes in the orthography of proper names from such Japanese texts as available, and who has assisted me out of various impasses where my own ignorance would have left me." (Noh, "Note") We do not know the extent of help Pound received from Waley, except in one play, Genjo, where Pound gives a footnote: "Note supplied by A.D.W. [Arthur Waley]" (Noh, p. 136). Whatever Waley's assistance may have been, there are still a number of significant errors, misunderstandings and omissions. Here again, even with the material available at Beinecke Library, we cannot always tell who is responsible, Fenollosa or Pound, except for a few places where Pound makes it clear that he either left ambiguity as it was because he did not understand, or interpreted a passage as he thought best. Nevertheless, it is Ezra Pound who completed the "translation" of these Noh plays. We may, therefore, assume that Pound is responsible for the artistic value of the finished form of the translation which we have now in print.

Pound's letters written after the publication of Noh show that he was not completely satisfied with his work. In a letter to John Quinn, Pound writes: "I find Noh unsatisfactory. I daresay it's all that could be done with the material. I don't believe anyone else will come along to do a better book on Noh, save for encyclopaedizing the subject. . . I think I am justified in having spent the time I did on it, but not much more than that" (Letters, # 153. London, 4 June, 1918). In 1927, more than ten years after he published his translations, Pound discussed their revision in a letter to Glenn Hughes:

> I wonder if Iwasaki is trained in No or if you and he want to undertake revision of my redaction of Fenollosa's paper on the Noh (or No; better I think spelled with the "h" to avoid homograph with simple Murkn [sic] negative).
>
> Don't know whether you know the work (pub. by Macmillan, now out of print). I think Fenollosa did a lot that ought not to be lost. I had not the philological competence necessary for an ultimate version, but at the same time Mrs. F's conviction was that Fen. wanted it transd as literature not as philology.
>
> Whether it wd. be more bother than worth to go over it and correct errors, I know not. I might want to look over result and possibly re-revise, though judging by 3 Jap lady-poets, not to any gt. extent. General principle of not putting in mere words that occur in original when they contribute nothing to the SENSE of the translation.
>
> One wants a Jap on the job, and one wants a Jap who knows Noh. I shd. like to protect Fenollosa from sonzovbitches like -- and in general from the philologs who were impotent till Fen. showed the way (via y.v.t.) and who then swarmed in with inferior understandings.
>
> . . . . . , . . .
>
> At present it is the scattered fragments left by a dead man, edited by a man ignorant of Japanese. Naturally any sonvbitch who

knows a little Nipponese can jump on it or say
his flatfooted renderings are a safer guide to
the style of that country. (<u>Letters</u>, # 227.
Rapallo, 9 November, 1927)

But Pound never revised his translation, despite his
dissatisfaction.

    It is clear that Pound's knowledge of the Japanese
language and of the Noh plays was extremely limited
when he started to work on the materials Fenollosa
left. Pound refers to these deficiencies in a letter
to Katue Kitasono written in 1936, twenty years after
the publication of <u>Noh</u>: "You must not run away with
the idea that I <u>really</u> know enough to read Japanese or
that I can do more than spell out ideograms <u>very</u> slowly
with a dictionary. I had all Fenollosa's notes and the
results of what he had learned from Umewaka Minoro
[sic], Dr. Mori, Dr. Ariga. But since Tami Koume was
killed in that earthquake I have had no one to explain
the obscure passages or fill up the enormous gaps of my
ignorance" (<u>Letters</u>, # 307. Rapallo, 24 May, 1936).
Concerning the Noh plays, Pound seems to have read
something about them, possibly after he received the
Fenollosa manuscripts but before he actually started to
work on them. He writes in the "Introduction": "as I
look over that section of his papers which deals with
the Japanese Noh, <u>having read what others have written
in English about these plays</u>, I am in a position to say
definitely that Professor Fenollosa knew more of the
subject than any one who has yet written in our tongue"
[Italics mine] (<u>Noh</u>, p. 3). Though Pound does not say
what he read on the Noh plays "written in English,"[23]
his evaluation of Fenollosa's knowledge of the subject
is certainly appropriate. In fact, considering his
lack of knowledge and background on the subject, Pound
shows an excellent insight into and appreciation of the
nature of the Noh plays in his "Introduction" and notes
(although, here again, we cannot tell how much of the
insight and appreciation is owing to Fenollosa). Pound
remarks: "The Noh is unquestionably one of the great
arts of the world, and it is quite possibly one of the
most recondite" (<u>Noh</u>, p. 3). He goes on to say:

> The art of allusion, or this love of allusion
> in art, is at the root of the Noh . . . . In
> the Noh we find an art built upon the god-
> dance, or upon some local legend of spiritual
> apparition, or, later, on gestes of war and
> feats of history; and art of splendid posture,

or dancing and chanting and of acting that is
not mimetic . . . . It is a symbolic stage, a
drama of masks--at least they have masks for
spirits and gods and young women. It is a
theatre of which both Mr. Yeats and Mr. Craig
may approve. It is not, like our theatre, a
place where every fineness and subtlety must
give way. (<u>Noh</u>, p. 4)

At another place Pound writes: "the Noh has its unity in emotion. It has also what we may call Unity of Image. At least, the better plays are all built into the intensification of a single image: the red maple leaves and the snow flurry in Nishikigi, the pines in Takasago, the blue-grey waves and wave pattern in Suma Genji, the mantle of feathers in the play of that name, Hagoromo" (<u>Noh</u>, p. 27). And Pound further comments: "This intensification of the Image, this manner of construction, is very interesting to me personally, as an Imagiste, for we Imagistes knew nothing of these plays when we set out in our own manner. These plays are also an answer to a question that has several times been put to me: 'Could one do a long Imagiste poem, or even a long poem in vers libre?'" (<u>Noh</u>, p. 27, footnote). Pound's remark that "the better plays are all built into the intensification of a single Image" best applies to <u>Takasago</u> (this play is not included in the fifteen plays translated and published by Fenollosa and Pound) and <u>Hagoromo</u>. In the former, the pines (more accurately, the pine-tree) are at once a single, predominant image and the symbol of eternity and constancy of vow between husband and wife--the subject matter of the play. In the original text of <u>Takasago</u> the word "the pine-tree" ("matsu" in Japanese) appears thirty-three times, scattered throughout the play. Sometimes the word is used simply to signify the pine-tree as the physical object; several times it is used as a pun with a Japanese word "matsu" ("to wait"); and sometimes the word "the pine-tree" is used in a figurative sense--as a symbol of eternity. In the play the pine-tree is both physical and symbolical. The setting is at the sea-shore of Takasago with its famous pine-tree. In the play the origin of the pine-tree at Takasago and what it stands for (that is, eternity and constancy) are explained in the dialogue. In <u>Hagoromo</u>, the feather-mantle ("hagoromo") of the angel is the key image. It is present on the stage throughout the play. It creates the conflict between the angel, its proper owner, and the fisherman, its finder, who wishes to keep it as treasure but eventually returns it to the angel. In <u>Nishikigi</u> and <u>Suma Genji</u>, however, Pound's comment needs some qualification, for in these two plays, a single image does not dominate the whole play. Rather the playwrights use a single image effectively and impressively at a certain part (or parts), as <u>Suma Genji</u> uses the image of "the blue-grey waves and wave pattern" in its very last part. In <u>Nishikigi</u> "the red maple leaves" appear in the middle of the play and "the snow flurry" toward the end.[24] The degree of the "intensification" of these images in this play, however, is much less than that of the images of the other three plays mentioned above. Moreover, "the red maple leaves" is an inaccurate translation of the original, "momiji-ba somete," which does not mean, in this context, "the red maple leaves" but "the leaves have changed their colors."[25]

In another part of <u>Noh</u> Pound again stresses the importance of the image in the plays: "The reader must remember that the words are only one part of this art. The words are fused with the music and with the ceremonial dancing. One must read or 'examine' these texts 'as if one were listening to music.' One must build out of their indefiniteness a definite image. The plays are at their best, I think, an image; that is to say, their unity lies in the image--they are built up about it as the Greek plays are built up about a single moral conviction" (<u>Noh</u>, p. 37). In reference to the play <u>Kakitsubata</u> Pound appropriately characterizes the Noh plays as an art of suggestion and implication, rather than that of explicit presentation: "The emotional tone [of <u>Kakitsubata</u>] is perhaps apparent. The spirit manifests itself in that particular iris marsh because Narihira in passing that place centuries before had thought of her [Kakitsubata, the heroine of the play]. Our own art is so much an art of emphasis, and even of over-emphasis, that it is difficult to consider the possibilities of an absolutely unemphasized art, an art where the author trusts so implicitly that his auditor will know what things are profound and important" (<u>Noh</u>, p. 130).

Although the translations of the Noh plays were not the most significant or the most influential[26] among the materials Pound found in the Fenollosa manuscripts, Pound did use his knowledge of the Noh plays in some of his prose works and, more significantly, in the <u>Cantos</u>.[27] In <u>Guide to Kulchur</u>[28] Pound writes:

. . . Fenollosa is said to have been the
second European to be able to take part in Noh
performance. The whole civilization reflected
in Noh is a high civilization.

   The ghost of Kumasaka [the principal
character of the play Kumasaka] returns not
from a grudge and not to gain anything; but to
state clearly that the very young man who had
killed him had not done so by a fluke or slip,
but that he had out-fenced him.

   The play Kagekiyo has Homeric
robustness. The Noh is not merely painting on
silk or nuances à la Chas. Condor.²⁹

   I pointed out in Noh that we err very
often in supposing that our system of
categories is the only possible kind. A
persian rug-maker can have colour categories
finer than ours. You must see what the other
fellow is using as demarcation before assuming
him vague or muddled.³⁰

In the Cantos Pound uses several Noh plays in various
places in various ways. The plays are: Aoi no Ue
(sometimes spelled "Awoi no Uye") (77/465, 110/780,
110/781); Suma Genji (74/443); Hagoromo (74/430,
79/485, 80/500); Kagekiyo (74/442); Kumasaka (74/442,
79/485); Kayoi Komachi or Sotoba Komachi (110/781); and
Takasago (4/15).³¹ The earliest reference to the Noh
plays in the Cantos is to Takasago in the following
section:

   Thus the light rains, thus pours, e lo soleils
                                         plovil
   The liquid and rushing crystal
      beneath the knees of the gods.
   Ply over ply, thin glitter of water;
   Brook film bearing white petals.
   The pine at Takasago
      grows with the pine of Iseĺ
   The water whirls up the bright pale sand in
                                the spring's mouth
   "Behold the Tree of the Visages!"
   Forked branch-tips, flaming as if with lotus.
      Ply over Ply
   The shallow eddying fluid,
      beneath the knees of the gods.   (4/15)

"The Pine at Takasago" does not seem to have any
further significance than as an image--the beautiful
pine tree along the shore of Takasago, juxtaposed with
the equally famous pine at Ise, the site of the Shinto
shrine.

There are three references to Hagoromo in the
Cantos. The first appears in the following section:

> a man on whom the sun has gone down
> the ewe, he said had such a pretty look in her
>   eyes;
> and the nymph of the Hagoromo came to me,
>   as a corona of angels
> one day were clouds banked on Taishan
>   or in glory of sunset
>   and tovarish blessed without aim
> wept in the rainditch at evening
>   Sunt lumina   (74/430)

The use of punctuation makes Pound's intention here
rather ambiguous, but "the nymph of the Hagoromo" is an
obvious reference to the main character of the play.
The next line may be meant to carry on the image of the
previous line to what follows. In the play she calls
herself a "sky-traversing spirit" and a "heaven-born"
maiden, living in heaven, and more specifically,
serving the goddess of the moon. The play has such
lines as:

> Upon a thousand heights had gathered the
>   inexplicable cloud.
> Swept by the rain, the moon is just come to light
>   the high house.[32] (Noh, p. 98)

It seems, then, that Pound uses the play Hagoromo and
its heroine, an angel, in this section, because the
atmosphere the play presents and the association with
heaven and light the play has are appropriate to this
section of the Cantos, which contains such images as
"the sun," "clouds," "glory of sunset," "evening" and
"lumina" (lights).

The second reference to Hagoromo is as follows:

> as the young horse whinnies against the tubas
>   in contending for certain values
> (Janequin per esempio, and Orazio Vechii or
>   Bronzino)

>   Greek rascality against Hagoromo
>   Kumasaka vs/ vulgarity
>   no sooner out of Troas
>   than the damn fools attacked Ismarus of the
>   Cicones   (79/485)

This section contains two references to the Noh plays: <u>Hagoromo</u> and <u>Kumasaka</u>. Apparently, Pound contrasts the purity and innocence of the angel in <u>Hagoromo</u> (the qualities the play emphasizes) to "Greek rascality," referring probably to the Greek treachery involved in the destruction of Troy and the whole mythos of their gods. Kumasaka is the name of the principal character of the play, and it seems that his virtue represented true nobility to Pound; hence Kumasaka is juxtaposed with "vulgarity."

The third reference to <u>Hagoromo</u> appears in the following section:

> The young Dumas weeps because the young Dumas
>   has tears
>   Death's seeds move in the year
>   semina motuum
>   falling back into the trough of the sea
>   the moon's arse been chewed off by this
>   time
> semina motuum
>   "With us there is no deceit"
>   said the moon nymph immacolata
>   Give back my cloak, <u>hagoromo</u>.
>   had I the clouds of heaven
>   as the nautile borne ashore
>   in their holocaust
>   as wistaria floating shoreward
>   with the sea gone the colour of copper
>   and emerald dark in the offing
> the young Dumas has tears thus far from the year's
>   end   (80/500)

The quotation is directly from the speech of the angel in <u>Hagoromo</u>: "Doubt is of mortals; with us there is no deceit." (<u>Noh</u>, p. 102) In the play, the angel's feathermantle, or cloak ("hagoromo"), is temporarily stolen by a fisherman who wants to keep it as a rare treasure, knowing that it belongs to the angel. The angel asks him to return her mantle. Hence "Give back my cloak, <u>hagoromo</u>." Since the play emphasizes the pure and innocent character of the angel, who serves

17

the moon goddess, Pound's description, "the moon nymph immacolata ["immaculate"]," is appropriate.

The second reference to Kumasaka (the first one is in [79/485], discussed above) is in the following section:

> wd/ have put the old man, son père on his shoulders
>   and gone off to some barren seacoast
> Says the Japanese sentry :   Paaak yu djeep over
>   there,
> some of the best soldiers we have says the captain
>   Dai Nippon Banzai from the Philippines
> remembering Kagekiyo :   "how stiff the shaft of
>   your neck is."
>   and they went off each his own way
> "a better fencer than I was," said Kumasaka, a
>   shade,
> "I believe in the resurrection of Italy   quia
>   impossible est
> 4 times to the song of Gassir
>   now in the mind indestructible   (74/442)

This passage has two references to the Noh plays: one to Kumasaka and the other to Kagekiyo. As for the reference to Kumasaka, Kumasaka's words quoted here, "better fencer than I was," are not in Pound's translation of the play, but the original text has the following passage which appears to correspond to the quotation: "I am no match for him in swordsmanship"—the implication is that Kumasaka's opponent is "a better fencer than [he] was." Thus, the quotation refers to Kumasaka's foe, Ushiwaka, a young boy who killed Kumasaka.[33] It seems that Pound refers to Kumasaka in this section for two reasons. First, though Kumasaka is not a soldier but a thief, he dies, fighting with Ushiwaka. At his death, Kumasaka is angry to have to die in the hand of such a young boy as Ushiwaka, but after death, Kumasaka's ghost appears and makes it clear that Ushiwaka's victory was proper and just because of his superior skill. In other words, Pound seems to admire the character of Kumasaka, who returns to do justice to his victor after his death. Secondly, the play, particularly its last part describing the fight between Kumasaka and Ushiwaka, appears to have impressed Pound considerably. Pound's remarks at the beginning of his translation of the play seem to justify this interpretation. Pound writes: "The final passage is the Homeric presentation of combat between him [Kumasaka] and the young boy,

Ushiwaka. But note here the punctilio. Kumasaka's spirit returns to do justice to the glory of Ushiwaka and to tell of his own defeat" (<u>Noh</u>, p. 38). As for the reference to <u>Kagekiyo</u>, the quotation, "how stiff the shaft of your neck is," is from the part of the chorus: "And Kagekiyo [the principal character of the play; a warrior] called at him. 'How tough the shaft of your neck is!' And they both laughed out over the battle, and went off each his own way" (<u>Noh</u>, p. 111). In his translation, Pound has "How tough. . ." rather than "how stiff. . ." Kagekiyo, now an old blind man, was once a brave warrior, as the chorus in another part of Pound's translation says: "Upon all the boats of the men of Heike's faction/ Kagekiyo was the fighter most in call" (<u>Noh</u>, p. 110). Thus, in this section of the <u>Cantos,</u> Pound apparently associates the Japanese soldiers with two brave fighters of the two Noh plays.

The reference to <u>Suma Genji</u> appears in the following section:

> in this air as of Kuanon
> enigma forgetting the times and seasons
> but this air brought her ashore a la marina
> with the great shell borne on the seawaves
>   nautilis biancastra
> By no means an orderly Dantescan rising
> but as the winds veer
>   tira libeccio
> now Genji at Suma   ,tira libeccio
>   as the winds veer and the raft is driven
>   and the voices   ,Tiro, Alcmene
>   with you is Europa nec casta Pasiphae
>   Eurus, Apeliota as the winds veer in
>   periplum
> Io son la luna" . . .   (74/443)

This section contains words and images related to the great goddess, Venus, to her force, and to the force of the sea and the sky. The scene is like that in Botticelli's painting of Venus rising from the sea: "air"; "ashore"; "a la marina" (in the naval manner); "the great shell"; "the seawaves"; "nautilis biancastra" (a white-colored shell); "winds"; "tira libeccio" (the south-west wind blows); "raft"; "Eurus" (the east, or south-east, wind); "Apeliota" (the East Wind); "Io son la luna" (I am the moon). As we have seen,[34] the play <u>Suma Genji</u> impressed Pound with its images of "the blue-grey waves and wave pattern." The setting of the play is along the shore of Suma, and

Genji, the principal character (who is also the hero of the Tale of Genji by Lady Murasaki, on which the play is based), is glorified in this play as a god-figure descending from heaven to save the mortals. And the play also has such lines as:

Genji:
> How beautiful this sea is! When I trod the grass here I was called 'Genji the gleaming', and now from the vaulting heaven I reach down to set a magic on mortals. I sing of the moon in this shadow, here on this sea-marge of Suma. Here I will dance Seikai-ha, the blue dance of the sea waves.

Chorus:
> The flower of waves-reflected
> Is on his white garment;
> That pattern covers the sleeve.
> The air is alive with flute-sounds,
> With the song of various pipes
> The land is a-quiver,
> And even the wild sea of Suma
>
> Is filled with resonant quiet.
> Moving in clouds and in rain,
> The dream overlaps with the real;
> There was a light out of heaven,
> There was a young man at the dance here;
> Surely it was Genji Hikaru,
> It was Genji Hikaru in spirit.
> . . . .

Chorus:
> He came down like Brahma, Indra, and the Four Kings visiting the abode of Devas and Men.
> . . . .
> Blue-grey is the garb they wear here,
> Blue-grey he fluttered in Suma;
> His sleeves were like the grey sea-waves;
> They moved with curious rustling,
> Like the noise of the restless waves,
> . . . .   (Noh, pp. 24-26)

Furthermore, Tiro, Alcmene, Europa and Pasiphae are all female characters in Greek mythology who are involved in illicit love affairs.[35] And Genji also has love affairs with many women. Genji beautifies the landscape as Venus and the women mentioned might. Thus, as in the case of the first reference to

Hagoromo, in this section, Pound seems to use the play Suma Genji for its atmosphere, situation and images appropriate to this part of the Cantos.

The first reference to Aoi no Ue is in the following section:

>   As Arcturus passes over my smoke-hole
>   the excess electric illumination
>   is now focussed
>   on the bloke who stole a safe he cdn't open
>   (interlude entitled: periplum by camion)
>   and Awoi's hennia   plays hob in the tent
>   flaps
>   k-lakk..... thuuuuuu
>   making rain
>   uuuh   (77/465)

Awoi (also spelled "Aoi") is the character in the play Aoi no Ue, whom Pound mistakenly believes to be the principal character.[36] Thus, to be correct, "Awoi's hennia" should be "Princess Rokujo's hannya"--Princess Rokujo is the principal character; and "hennia" is more correctly spelled "hannya," an evil spirit in Noh drama. The "witch" is simply a personification of the wind moving tent flaps in Pound's vicinity at the Pisan cage. It is difficult to see much significance in the reference to the play Aoi no Ue in this part of the Cantos. In the play, there is an allusion to an incident which involved Princess Rokujo and Aoi while they were in their respective carriages. If Pound means a "dray" by "camion," he may have associated the "camion" with the alluded incident in the play.

The second reference to Aoi no Ue occurs in Canto CX:

>   That love be the cause of hate,
>   something is twisted,
>   Awoi,
>   bare trees walk on the sky-line,
>   but that one valley reach the four seas,
>   mountain sunset inverted   (CX/780)
>
>   The marble form in the pine wood,
>   The shrine seen and not seen
>   From the roots of sequoias
>   敬   ching[4]
>   pray   pray
>   There is power

21

Awoi or Komachi,
          the oval moon. (CX/781)

As in the case of an earlier reference to Aoi in 77/465, here in these two passages, we seem to detect Pound's misunderstanding of the play Aoi no Ue. In the first example above, Pound's interpretation of Aoi as the principal character of the play who is tormented by her own jealousy,[37] seems to be carried through in his juxtaposition of "Awoi" and "That love be the cause of hate." The second example is more obscure. "Komachi" may be Ono no Komachi, the main character of two plays, Sotoba Komachi and Kayoi Komachi, which are among the fifteen Noh plays translated by Pound. She is famous for her beauty and poetic talent as well as for her haughty rejection of many suitors. In both plays (as in many Noh plays) the spirit of Komachi, who has long been dead, appears in a human form. Thus, if we take into consideration Pound's misunderstanding of Aoi as "a phantom or image of Awoi no Uye's own jealousy" (Noh, p. 114), we can see that Aoi and Komachi are placed together because, for Pound, they have something in common: that they are both "phantoms" or "wraiths" (the word "wraith" appears on p. 779). For an interpretation of the connection between "power," "Awoi or Komachi" (or the implication of their being "wraiths"), and "The oval moon" (possibly suggestive of illumination or light, and further, of perception), I would like to refer to Professor Nassar's comment on "Drafts and Fragments 1968" in his book, The Cantos of Ezra Pound: The Lyric Mode.[38] The point to be made here is that, as Professor Terrell suggests, in Canto CX, Pound carried his misunderstanding of the play Aoi no Ue into this context.

    In concluding this chapter, we may summarize the significance of the Noh plays to Pound. Pound approached Noh virtually as a stranger at the time when he was chosen to be Ernest Fenollosa's literary executor. His job, among others, was to complete Fenollosa's unfinished translation of the Noh plays into English. Despite considerable linguistic deficiencies, Pound soon perceived certain basic qualities of Noh, such as its suggestiveness, its allusions, its use of the symbolic stage and masks, and the most important of all to Pound the Imagiste, its effective use of certain images, or as he calls it, the "intensification of the Image." It seems as though Pound found the validity and justification of his theory of the Imagisme in the Noh plays. However, Noh never became a major influence on Pound, as did the Chinese materials which were also in the Fenollosa manuscripts, and in which Pound became deeply and enormously interested. Pound once said: "China is fundamental, Japan is not." Although he found both China and Japan in Fenollosa's literary remains, for Pound the former was far more interesting and significant. It is true that he did use Noh in the <u>Cantos</u>, but the importance of Noh in this work is, as we have seen, no more than providing separate sections of the poem with fragmentary images, and less frequently, atmospheres and feelings. In the next two chapters, I will discuss the Noh plays themselves which Pound translated.

Notes to Chapter I

1. Kan'ami, or Kanze Kiyotsugu (1333-1383). Zeami, or Kanze Motokiyo (1363-1443). Zeami is considered the greatest writer of Noh. He was an actor as well as a playwright. He also left important commentary and criticism of the Noh plays.

2. Arthur Waley, The No Plays of Japan (New York: Grove Press, Inc., 1957), p. 17. Further page references will be made in parentheses following quotations from this text, hereafter identified as Waley.

3. Hisashi Furukawa, Noh no Sekai ["The World of Noh"], (Tokyo: Shakai Shiso-sha, 1960), pp. 51-116.

4. The auxiliary verb soro, when added to main verbs of a sentence, makes the main verbs either honorific (the speaker showing respect for another character) or humble (the speaker showing modesty and humility), depending on the context.

5. For Pound's handling of the style, see Appendix I.

6. Ise Monogatari is the oldest utamonogatari (a poetic tale, or a tale consisting of many waka, or a Japanese verse form of thirty-one syllables) in Heian period. Love is the main theme. Neither the author nor the exact date is known (c. 950?).

7. Ernest F. Fenollosa, Epochs of Chinese and Japanese Art: An Outline History of East Asiatic Design [New and revised edition, with copious notes by Professor Petrucci], (New York: Dover Publications, Inc., 1963), Vol. I, p. xiv.

8. Ibid.

9. Ibid., p. xxviii.

10. Ibid., p. xvi.

11. Charles Norman explains the circumstances: "For a number of years, Mrs. Ernest Fenollosa. . . had been on the lookout for a writer to whom she could entrust her husband's translations and notes. 'Contemporania' [a series of Pound's poems published in

Poetry (April 1913) under that general heading]
convinced her that Pound was the man. . ." (Charles
Norman, Ezra Pound [New York: The Macmillan Co.,
1960], p. 99.) The editor of Ezra Pound: Perspectives
writes: "Mrs. Fenollosa, after seeing some of Ezra
Pound's verse in Poetry, decided he was the person best
fitted to take charge of her husband's literary rmains
and handed them over to him, in London, toward the end
of 1913. . ." (Ezra Pound: Perspectives, ed. Noel
Stock [Chicago: Henry Regnery Co., 1965], p. 177.)
Concerning Mrs. Fenollosa's intention, Pound himself
explains in his letter to Glenn Hughes as quoted in Ch.
1, p. 11.

12. A Hindu poet and reformer, lecturer on social,
religious, and educational topics, and first woman
governor of an Indian province. 1879-1949.

13. Ezra Pound & Ernest Fenollosa, The Chinese
Written Character as a Medium for Poetry. [and]
Confucius. The Unwobbling Pivot & The Great Digest,
(New York: Kasper & Horton, [no date]), p. 4.
Also, Noel Stock notes that a similar information is
found in Pound's B.B.C. broadcasts in 1959. (Noel
Stock, Poet in Exile: Ezra Pound [New York: Barnes &
Noble, Inc., 1964], p. 75.)

14. Ezra Pound, Selected Letters of Ezra Pound
1907-1941, ed. D. D. Paige (New York: New Directions,
1971), #31. 19 December, 1913. Further references
will be made in parentheses following quotations from
this text, hereafter identified as Letters.

15. Ezra Pound, EP to LU: Nine Letters Written to
Louis Untermeyer by Ezra Pound, ed. J. A. Robbins.
(Bloomington, Indiana: Indiana University Press,
1963), # 1.

16. Stock, Poet in Exile: Ezra Pound, pp. 75-76.

17. Professor Hugh Kenner refers to some of the
Fenollosa manuscripts which exist or existed at
Brunnenberg in his Pound Era (Berkeley and Los
Angeles: University of California Press, 1971), p.
573. It is not known whether or not the holdings at
Beinecke Library represent all that was at
Brunnenberg. Additionally, the microfilm titled
"Fenollosa Diaries" housed at the University of
Virginia contains no material directly pertinent to the
translations of Noh plays.

18. For example, most pages are handwritten but not necessarily by Fenollosa, while some are typed; for some plays, both the Japanese text (transliterated in English alphabet) and its English translation are given, while for others, only the translation is provided. The kind of translation is not uniform, either. For two or three plays, both a very rough literal translation and a more smooth, more "finished" version are given, while in most other cases, either a very rough literal translation or a slightly more finished rendering alone is given.

19. In retrospect, Pound tells us what Fenollosa's work meant to him and to his literary career in Make It New: "Fenollosa's work was given me in manuscript when I was ready for it. It saved me a great deal of time. It saved probably less time to a limited number of writers who noticed it promptly but who didn't live with it as closely as I did. Fenollosa died in 1908. I began an examination of comparative European literature in or about 1901; with the definite intention of finding out what had been written, and how. The motives I presumed to differ with the individual writers." (Ezra Pound, Make It New: Essays by Ezra Pound [New Haven: Yale University Press, 1935], p. 8.)

20. Before the publication of the translation of the Noh plays, Pound published Cathay as the first product of his work on the Fenollosa manuscripts in 1915. The complete title of Cathay reads:

Cathay. Translations by Ezra Pound. For the most part from the Chinese of Rihaku, from the notes of the late Ernest Fenollosa, and the decipherings of the professors Mori and Ariga. (Ezra Pound, Cathay, [London: Elkin Mathews, 1915].)

In March 1916, Pound writes in his letter to Kate Buss:

Further announcement:

> CERTAIN NOBLE PLAYS OF JAPAN
> FROM THE MANUSCRIPTS OF ERNEST FENOLLOSA
> SELECTED AND FINISHED BY EZRA POUND
> WITH AN INTRODUCTION BY W. B. YEATS

Now being published by the Cuala Press (10/6). I expect proofs any day. I dare say they'll send you a review copy if you write to them for it. ----But if you want "copy" you'd better save it for an article on the new theatre, or theatreless drama, about which there'll be a good deal to say soon, as Yeats is making new start on the foundation of these Noh dramas. (<u>Letters</u>, # 84. London, 9 March, 1916)

21. In 1959 the book was published in paperbook form by New Directions under the title: <u>The Classic Noh Theatre of Japan</u>. For my study I have used this New Directions edition, sixth printing. Hereafter, the text, which has been published thus under three different titles, will be identified as <u>Noh</u>. The page references will be made in parentheses following quotations from this text.

22. Teele, p. 169.

23. Although we do not know what Pound read on the Noh plays, there are several writings which he might have read. Marie C. Stopes gives the following list, to which her own book should be added:
Aston, W.G. <u>A History of Japanese Literature</u>. Heinemann, London, 1899.
Brinkley, F. <u>Japan: its History, Arts and Literature</u>, Vol. iii. London, 1903.
Chamberlain, B.H. <u>The Classical Poetry of the Japanese</u>. Boston, 1880. Reprinted with additions and deletions as <u>Japanese Poetry</u>, London, 1911.
Dickins, F.V. <u>Primitive and Mediaeval Japanese Texts translated into English</u>. Oxford, 1906.
Edwards, O. <u>Japanese Plays and Playfellows</u>. London, 1901.
Sansom, G.B. "Translations from Lyrical Drama: 'No.'" <u>Trans. Asiatic Soc</u>. Japan, 1911, vol. 38, part 3.
Stopes, M.C. "A Japanese Mediaeval Drama," <u>Trans. Royal Soc. Literature</u>, London, 1909, vol. 29, part 3.
(Stopes, Marie C., <u>Plays of Old Japan: The 'No'</u>. [New York, 1913], p. 103, "English Bibliography of the <u>No</u>.")

24. In Part II of <u>Nishikigi</u>, the first two lines of the old woman's second speech read: "Our hearts have been in the dark of the falling snow, / We have been astray in the flurry" (<u>Noh</u>, p. 83). These two lines contain the image of "snow" and "flurry."

However, in the original text, there are no words for either "snow" or "flurry." A more literal translation of the original corresponding to these two lines reads: "Our hearts are in turmoil with the passions of love."

25. The word "momiji-ba" can mean "the red maple leaves" in a different context, but not here.

26. Pound's interest in the Chinese materials was far greater. Out of the Fenollosa materials Pound published two important works: Cathay and The Chinese Written Character as a Medium for Poetry. Comparing Japan and China, Pound writes in a letter to John Quinn: ". . . China is fundamental, Japan is not. Japan is a special interest, like Provence, or 12-13th Century Italy (apart from Dante). I don't mean to say there aren't interesting things in Fenollosa's Japanese stuff (or fine things, like the end of Kagekiyo [one of the Noh plays Pound translated], which is, I think, 'Homeric'). But China is solid. One can't go back of the 'Exile's Letter,' or the 'Song of the Bowmen,' or the 'North Gate'" (Letters, # 115. 10 January, 1917). To Pound, the Fenollosa manuscripts were the most powerful introduction to the Chinese, especially Confucian, system of ideas, in which Pound has been greatly interested ever since, and which occupies an important place in his Cantos.

27. The Cantos of Ezra Pound, (New York: New Directions, 1972).

28. Besides Guide to Kulchur, there is one reference to the Noh plays in ABC of Reading: ". . . a Japanese emperor whose name I have forgotten and whose name you needn't remember, found that there were TOO MANY NOH PLAYS, he picked out 450 and the Noh stage LASTED from 1400 or whenever right down till the day the American navy intruded, and that didn't stop it. Umewaka Minoru started again as soon as the revolution wore off. . ." (Ezra Pound, ABC of Reading [New York: New Directions, 1960], p. 92) The first half of this passage is not based on any recorded history of the Noh plays, although the last half is generally correct.

29. Ezra Pound, Guide to Kulchur, (New York: New Directions, [1952] [first published 1938]), p. 81.

30. Ibid., p. 166.

31. (4/15) signifies Canto 4, page 15. The Annotated Index to the Cantos includes all the titles of the first five plays, identifying each as a Noh play translated by Pound. Neither Kayoi Komachi nor Sotoba Komachi appears in the Index, since the Index covers Cantos 1 through 84 only. The last play, Takasago, is not identified as the title of a Noh play but merely as a place name in the Index. (We may note here that Takasago is not one of the fifteen plays included in Noh.) It is true that "Takasago" is a place name in Japan, famous for the pines, but it is also the title of a play, the setting of which is at Takasago, and in which the pine-tree is a predominant image. From his comment in Noh (quoted on p. 22), we can assume that Pound uses the name "Takasago," knowing it both as a place name and as the title of a Noh play. But A Companion to the Cantos of Ezra Pound identifies "Takasago" both as the play title and as a place name. See Carroll F. Terrell, A Companion to the Cantos of Ezra Pound, Vol. I (Cantos 1 - 71), (Berkeley, Los Angeles, London: University of California Press, 1980), p. 13.

32. The two lines quoted above are an inaccurate translation of the original, which reads like this:

Over the lovely mountain thousands of miles
  away suddenly arose the cloud;
But the bright moon shone upon the
  tower as the rain cleared off.

33. See Pound's comment on Kumasaka in Guide to Kulchur, quoted on p. 15.

34. See p. 14.

35. Tiro [Tyro] bore twin sons to Poseidon (the god of the sea); Alcmene bore Heracles by Zeus and Iphicles by Amphitryon; Europa was courted and captured by Zeus, who assumed the form of a bull; and Poseidon made Pasiphae fall in love with a bull to punish her husband, Minos, King of Crete--hence she is called "casta Pasiphae" (chaste Pasiphae).

36. See the discussion of Pound's version of Aoi no Ue, Ch. II.

37. See Ch. II for further discussion.

38. Eugene Paul Nassar, *The Cantos of Ezra Pound: The Lyric Mode* (Baltimore and London: The Johns Hopkins University Press, 1975), pp. 136-142.

CHAPTER II

EZRA POUND'S VERSION OF THE NOH PLAYS

(1) INTRODUCTION

There are several problems in any comparison of Ezra Pound's "translations" of the Noh plays with the originals. We have already pointed out two such problems in the previous chapter: (1) that Noh is the work of at least three men: Hirata Kiichi, Ernest Fenollosa and Ezra Pound, and that we cannot decide exactly what part each of these three men is responsible for, because those Fenollosa manuscripts which are made public at Beinecke Library are not complete; and (2) that, consequently, we cannot always tell who is responsible for the errors, misunderstandings and omissions in the published work, except for a few places where Pound acknowledges his own interpretations or changes made in the original Fenollosa manuscripts. We decided, however, that Pound is responsible for the final form of the translation since he accepted and completed the task started by Fenollosa. There is yet a third problem: we do not know on which text Fenollosa based his rough translation of the Noh plays. Today there are five schools of Noh--Kanze, Komparu, Hojo, Kongo and Kita-- and each school has its own texts compiled according to its own interpretation. Thus, there are often considerable variations among the texts of a single Noh play. The main part of a play, however, remains the same in the texts of different schools. Concerning this textual problem, I agree with Professor Teele, who says:

> . . . Without being certain what Japanese text Fenollosa used, detailed criticism is difficult. It would be reasonable to use the Kwanze ["Kwanze" is often spelled "Kanze"] texts, since Fenollosa studied with Umewaka Minoru, and the Umewaka school of noh singing is traditionally related to the Kwanze school (and in fact is at present included within that school, though for some decades it was independent).[1]

In spite of these difficulties, in the following pages I shall make a comparative study of Ezra Pound's version of the Noh plays with the original Japanese texts, mostly, of the Kanze school.[2]

(2) SOTOBA KOMACHI

The play is based on the legend of Ono no Komachi (either "Ono" or "Komachi" is used as a shortened form of the name, although the latter is more commonly used among Japanese), known as an excellent poet and a woman of matchless beauty in her youth (c. 850), who scornfully rejected many lovers. Among them was Shii no Shosho, who was told to make one hundred nightly visits to her house if his desire was to be fulfilled. He made ninety-nine nocturnal trips, but on the last night he died. In her old age, Ono lived in loneliness and destitution. The play opens with the appearance of two travelling priests from Koyasan who express the mental state of one who has renounced the world. Then Komachi, now a wandering old hag, appears and sits on the sotoba (stupa in Sanskrit; "a carved wooden devotional stick, or shrine" [Noh, p. 13]) to rest. One of the priests scolds her for her lack of respect toward Buddha, for the sotoba represents the sacred form of Buddha. Komachi immediately talks back to the priest and a disputation over the sotoba between the priest and Komachi takes place, and ends with Komachi's victory. Then the priest asks who the woman is, and she tells him that she is the ruin of the famous beauty, Ono no Komachi, and contrasts the kind of life she is living now (that is, as a beggar) with that of her brilliant youth. Suddenly Komachi becomes mad, possessed by the spirit of Shosho (who died as an unsuccessful suitor to Komachi). In her madness, the story of Shosho's having come to Komachi for a hundred nights but one is told. The play ends with the chorus persuading Komachi to try to attain Buddhahood through prayer.

There is a shift in the main interest of the play between the first and the second half. In the first half, the main action is the religious disputation betweeen Komachi and priests. In appearance, two different religious viewpoints are presented. However, the play's real interest is Komachi's wit and sophistry in religious disputation. In the second half, the focus is on the vicissitudes of human affairs--what has become of a once proud and beautiful woman. Toward the end of the play Komachi is temporarily possessed by the spirit of Shosho, but neither Fenollosa nor Pound seems to have understood this fact.

One major problem of Pound's version of <u>Sotoba Komachi</u> is that as far as the length of the play is concerned, Pound's translation presents only about a fifth of the original text. Pound's text has 46 lines, whereas the original play in Arthur Waley's translation[3] has 229 lines. Due to these heavy cuts, Pound's version--although it presents the plot sufficiently--fails to include some of the important and interesting aspects and characteristics of the original play. This failing is most notable in the absence of almost all the references to Buddhist doctrines which the original text contains. As an example, let us consider Pound's handling of the opening part of the play. In the original, before the appearance of Komachi, two priests appear and introduce themselves. In his version, Pound gives the summary of the first part of the play in the form of a headnote, in which he also explains who Ono no Komachi is: "Thus, in Sotoba Komachi, a play by Kiyotsugu, two priests are going from Koyosan [Koyasan] to Kioto [Kyoto], and in Settsu they meet with Ono no Komachi; that is to say, they meet with what appears to be an old woman sitting on a roadside shrine [sotoba]--though she is really the wraith of Ono, long dead" (<u>Noh</u>, p. 13). Pound's note, however, does not tell the fact that the initial dialogue between the two priests (which Pound leaves out entirely) deals with Buddhist concepts of Buddhahood, incarnation and the essential meaninglessness of life in this world.

In some places which have religious references in the original, Pound's translation--when he does translate such parts--is not adequate. For example, the priest's second speech shows that Pound (or Fenollosa) misunderstood the original text, which reads as follows:

> Even the decayed tree in remote mountains
> Can be known from the blossoms it has put on;
> Then how could this tree
> Which has been carved as an embodiment of
> Buddha's body
> Be without its marvelous power?

Compare this to Pound's version: "Is it only a stick or a stump? Maybe it had once fine flowers--in its time, in its time; and now it is a stick, to be sure, with the blessed Buddha cut in it" (<u>Noh</u>, p. 13). Obviously, Pound or Fenollosa misunderstood the original meaning of the passage. The original text stresses the point that no matter how the form or shape may change, the sacred power within will remain unchanged. Pound's version, on the other hand, fails to present the point. Instead, it stresses the changes in the form the tree has undergone, rather than the inner power which is unchanged.

Following this speech, Komachi replies, according to Pound's version: "Oh, well then, I'm a stump, too, and well buried, with a flower at my heart. Go on and talk of the shrine" (Noh, p. 13). Pound's "Go on and talk of the shrine" is not an adequate rendering of the original: "Why is this called Buddha's body?" This question raised by Komachi opens the disputation concerning the nature of the sotoba. This section explains, in the form of a dialogue (between the priests and Komachi with occasional participation by the chorus), certain Buddhist principles such as the efficacy of the sotoba, the dichotomy of flesh and soul, and the way toward salvation. Pound leaves out this portion (some fifty lines) completely, except for the inaccurate brief note: "The Tsure, in this case the second priest, tells the legend of the shrine" (Noh, p. 13).

This long religious disputation in the middle of the original serves a double purpose: to show not only two different religious viewpoints on the nature of the sotoba but also Komachi's intelligence, which greatly impresses the priests, in spite of some disrespestful remarks on her part. In other words, this section is important in Komachi's characterization. Thus, Pound's version loses an interesting and significant part of the original play.

At the end of the dialogue, one of the priests asks: "What kind of person are you? Please tell us your name." Pound's version presents this transition by a brief and ambiguous note: "and while he [the second priest] is doing it [telling 'the legend of the shrine'], the Waki [the first priest] notices something strange about the old hag, and cries out" (Noh, p. 13). Moreover, in Pound's version, the priest's question is simply: "Who are you?" Komachi's reply in the original is as follows: "Though I am ashamed, I shall tell you my name. I am a daughter of Ono no Yoshizane, Governor of the district of Dewa; I am the ruins of Ono no Komachi." Compare this to Pound's version, "I am the ruins of Ono,/ The daughter of Ono no Yoshizane." In the original, Komachi is asked to identify herself; she is not asked what kind of person she is "inwardly."

Because of its omissions, Pound's version[4] presents only the most important point of each part or each speech and excludes many of the elaborate expressions and metaphors that the original text contains. Quite often Pound condenses a long, intricate passage into a much shorter, unadorned one. In this limited sense, one may say that in Pound's version (of this play) the matter, not the manner, is more important. Komachi's initial speech is a good example. Pound condenses the original twenty-eight (in Waley's version) into just six lines, presenting only the main point of her speech. Pound's translation, aside from its being shorter than the original, does not convey the ornate expression of the original--one of the characteristics of a Noh play. In the original Komachi's voice is described in an elaborate manner:

> I spoke with the voice of a nightingale;
> My voice, indeed, was praised
> As being rarer and lovelier
> Than the petals of the itohagi [a name of a
>   flower],
> Moist with dew,
> Which are just beginning to fall.

Pound has: "I spoke like the nightingales." Needless to say, the economy of Pound's version is striking--the whole passage is reduced to less than one line. We do not know whether or not the half-line, "I spoke like the nightingales," appears in the Fenollosa manuscripts exactly as it is in Pound's version.[5] In other words, we do not know who is responsible for the reduction. At any rate, however, the translation, "I spoke like the nightingales," obviously fails to present the metaphor and the intricate manner in which the original text describes the quality of Komachi's voice.

One of the charms of the Noh play lies in the fact that playwrights often give the description of a character, or of a surrounding landscape in an exchange of one-line (or less) speeches between the characters, rather than in the form of a narrative by one character. In this play, where the original describes Komachi's clothing and belongings in a series of questions and answers between the chorus and Komachi, Pound gives the description in a straight narration, of

a much shorter length, spoken in unison by the two
priests. The section in question reads:

>   Chorus: What is it that you carry in the bag
>   strung at your neck?
>   Komachi: Though I know not if I live through
>   today,
>   In order to save me from hunger tomorrow
>   I carry in my bag dried beans and dried
>   millet.
>   Chorus: And in the bag on your back?
>   Komachi: My garment soiled in dust and sweat.
>   Chorus: And in the basket on your arm?
>   Komachi: White and black arrowheads.
>   Chorus: Tattered straw coat;
>   Komachi: Broken bamboo hat;
>   Chorus: You cannot even hide your face;
>   Komachi: How could I escape from frost, snow,
>   rain, and dew?

Pound reduces the passage to two lines spoken in unison
by the two priests:

>   The wallet about her throat has in it a few dried
>   beans,
>   A bundle is wrapped on her back, and on her
>   shoulder is a basket of woven roots. (Noh, p.
>   14)

Regrettably this destroys one of the charms and
distinguishing characteristics of a Noh play.

At the end of the speech spoken in unison by the
two priests in Pound's version, describing Komachi's
appearance and action (two lines of which are quoted
above), the reader is supposed to understand that the
spirit of Komachi's lover Shosho possesses her, and
that what she says in her "madness" is not really what
she says or means but what Shosho says through her.
Fenollosa or Pound failed to understand this
"possession scene."

Pound frankly admits that he does not understand
in his note: "I cannot quite make out whether the
priest is still skeptical, and thinks he has before him
merely an old woman who thinks she is Komachi. At any
rate, she does not want commiseration, and replies"
(Noh, p. 14). The last sentence of this note is
inadequate, for it is not Komachi, but Shosho who
actually speaks. Thus, Komachi's seemingly defiant

tone of speech in Pound's version of Komachi's fifth speech (with which Pound ends his version of the play) is not necessarily in her nature. Pound's version, however, suggests that Komachi's speech represents her nature, and that he interprets Komachi's character on that basis.

Pound's translation of Sotoba Komachi which ends with the eleven-line speech by Komachi is incomplete, for the ending is omitted. In the original, there are approximately sixty lines after Shosho possesses Komachi. Komachi's fifth speech in Pound's version is only a part of the final portion, in which the priest, Komachi and the chorus, all take part. As in the rest of Pound's version of this play, in the last portion (inaccurately assigned to Komachi) Pound condenses the original and presents only the main point. First, let us quote the passage in Pound's translation:

> Daft! Will you hear him? In my own young days
> I had a hundred letters from men a sight
> better than he is. They came like rain-drops
> in May. And I had a high head, may be, that
> time. And I sent out no answer. You think
> because you see me alone now that I was in
> want of a handsome man in the old days, when
> Shosho came with the others--Shii no Shosho
> of Fukakusa that came to me in the moonlight
> and in the dark night and in the nights
> flooded with rain, and in the black face of
> the wind and in the wild swish of the snow.
> He came as often as the melting drops fall
> from the eaves, ninety-nine times, and he
> died. And his ghost is about me, driving me
> on with madness. (Noh, pp. 14-15)

"Daft! Will you hear him?" at the beginning is not in the original. The next four sentences are close to the original. The next sentence, "You think because you see me alone now that I was in want of a handsome man in the old days, when Shosho came with the others," is considerably different from the original, which reads (Shosho speaking through Komachi): "And now she is a hundred years old/And lives in punishment./ I love her, oh I love her." This part is difficult to understand, if one does not know that Shosho's spirit, possessing Komachi, actually speaks. Thus, what she says in the "possession scene" does not represent her true character. Then the original has the priest interrupt: "You love her? Then, whose spirit has possessed you?"

Pound omits this interruption. The remaining part is a condensation of the original, which tells the story of Shosho's coming to Komachi for ninety-nine nights in vain, spoken alternately by Komachi (Shosho) and the chorus.

The original text ends with the chorus which recommends Komachi (who by that time is no longer possessed by Shosho's spirit) to pray for the life hereafter.

> From such an experience as this,
> One understands that the only true way is
> To pray for the life hereafter;
> By collecting sands to build a memorial tower;
> [By accumulating small good deeds as if]
> To burnish Buddha's body with gold;
> By dedicating flowers to Buddha;
> Let us enter the path of enlightenment.
> Let us enter the path of enlightenment.

Pound's translation shows neither the fact that Komachi's madness is broken, Shosho's spirit leaving her before the end of the play, nor the fact that the play emphasizes the soul's salvation.

(3) NISHIKIGI

The plot of the play is as follows: A travelling priest has come to Kyo, where he is asked by an old man and an old woman (who appear to be husband and wife) to buy "hosonuno" and "nishikigi" which are noted products of the place. The priest then asks what these two things signify. They explain:

> As the cloth Hosonuno is narrow of weft,
> More narrow than the breast,
> We call by this name any woman
> Whose breasts are hard to come nigh to.
> (<u>Noh</u>, p. 78)

And "nishikigi" is a wooden stick (about one foot long) which a man places at the gate of the woman's house whom he wishes to marry. If the stick is accepted, his suit is successful. If he is rejected, the stick will remain where it was placed. The couple then takes the priest to a hill called "Nishikizuka" (a hill of nishikigi), where there is the grave of a man who offered a stick every day to a woman for three years and died. The couple disappears into the grave. After that the priest prays for the two, and then falls asleep. In his dream the same couple appears and tells him a story of their past--the man is the unsuccessful suitor and the woman is the object of his love in the story just told. Then they dance with joy, for they are finally united (after death) through the priest's prayer. At dawn, the two disappear and the priest is awakened from his dream, at which point the play ends. The subject matter of the play is the unrequited love of a man for a woman, who however, after death, is united with her through the prayer of a priest.

Of the fifteen Noh plays which Pound translated, <u>Nishikigi</u> is the most thorough and complete translation of the original text. One conspicuous feature of Pound's translation of this play is the fact that his version is often longer than the original, because he adds words, phrases, even lines. The way in which he does this, and its effect, vary. First, he sometimes adds explanatory words. For example, Pound's version of the first speech spoken in unison by the old man and the old woman of Part I reads:[6] "Times out of mind am I here setting up this bright branch, this silky wood with the charms painted in it as fine as the web you'd get in the grass-cloth of Shinobu, that they'd be still selling you in this mountain" (Noh, p. 76). A more literal translation of the original (which is written in verse) reads like this:

> 'Tis the "hosonuno" cloth,
> Woven here in Kyo.
> And 'tis the famous "nishikigi"
> That men set up.

In addition to mentioning these two objects, Pound explains, in particular, what the "nishikigi" is, and also tells us that both products are sold. Pound's version, then, has, in appearance, little resemblance to the original, but it does not distort or misrepresent the sense of the original, merely changes it from verse to prose.

Secondly, Pound sometimes amplifies or paraphrases the original.[7] Pound's translation of the fourth chorus of Part I reads:

> And storms; trees giving up their leaf,   1
> Spotted with sudden showers.
> Autumn! our feet are clogged
> In the dew-drenched, entangled leaves.
> The perpetual shadow is lonely,   5
> The mountain shadow is lying alone.
> The owl cries out from the ivies
> That drag their weight on the pine.
> Among the orchids and chrysanthemum flowers
> The hiding fox is now lord of that love-cave,   10
> Nishidzuka [an error for "Nishikizuka"],
> That is dyed like the maple's leaf.[8]
> They have left us this thing for a saying.
> That pair has gone into the cave.   14
>   (Noh, p. 81)

The first line of the original, "The storm, cold gusts, and drizzling rain," corresponds to the first two and a half lines in Pound's translation (from the beginning to "Autumn!"). What Pound (or Fenollosa) does here is to translate literally the meaning of each Chinese character, but not necessarily the meaning of each word, into English. A word may consist of one or more than one Chinese character. For example, the word for "storms" consists of one Chinese character. Therefore, Pound's translation, "storms," in line 1, is correct. However, "trees giving up their leaf" is a paraphrase of two Chinese characters which, combined, mean "cold gusts." Thus, the last half of line 1 of Pound's version is inaccurate. By ignoring the fact that two characters combined make one word, Pound presents a translation which is both wordy and incorrect. Line 2, "Spotted with sudden showers," is an amplification of the original word meaning "drizzling rain." "Autumn" at the beginning of line 3 is not in the original. Lines 3-4, "our feet are clogged/In the dew-drenched, entangled leaves," are an elaboration of the original, "our feet are clogged in the dew-drenched leaves." The original, corresponding to lines 5-6, reads: "The perpetual mountain shadow is lying alone." Pound's two lines are repetitious. Lines 7-10 are a good translation. The original, corresponding to Pound's last four lines, reads:

> . . . Where the leaves have changed colors.
> Nishikizuka is here.
> So saying the pair has gone into the cave.

Thus, line 13 of Pound's version is an incorrect and inadequate elaboration of the original, "So saying."

Another example of elaboration is seen in Pound's version of the first speech of the old woman, in Part II. Pound's translation reads:

> Aie, honoured priest!   1
> You do not dip twice in the river
> Beneath the same tree's shadow
> Without bonds in some other life.
> Hear soothsay,   5
> Now is there meeting between us,
> Between us who were until now
> In life and in after-life kept apart.
> A dream-bridge over wild grass,
> Over the grass I dwell in.   10
> O honoured! do not awake me by force.
> I see that the law is perfect. (Noh, pp. 81-82)

Lines 7, 8 and 10 are not in the original. Pound seems to have added these lines as an explanation. Compare this to a more literal translation of the original:

> <u>Honoured priest</u>, we hear that
> <u>Without bonds in some other life</u>,
> One does not stay under a certain tree
> Or take a drink from a certain river.
> Much less common is the meeting between us.
> Do not disturb the dream for a while yet.
> <u>I see that the law is perfect</u>.

(Italics indicate the parts which agree with
Pound's translation.)

Sometimes Pound's translation is more poetic than the original. In the following example, we may say that Pound, while presenting the idea of the original properly, created a new poem out of the original text. A literal translation of the second speech of the old woman of Part II reads:

Our hearts are in turmoil with the passions of
love. Let the world decide whether it is a dream
or reality.

Compare this to Pound's translation:

Our hearts have been in the dark of the falling
   snow.
We have been astray in the flurry.
You should tell better than we
How much is illusion,
You who are in the world.
We have been in the whirl of those who are fading.
                                          (Noh, p. 83)

Although Pound's version shows that his understanding of the play is generally correct, there are three places where he either neglects or fails to present entirely the religious references. The first example is in the last six lines of the third chorus of Part I. Pound's translation reads:

Please set your mind on this matter.
   'You'd be asking where the dew is
   'While the frost's lying here on the road.
   'Who'd tell you that now?'
Very well, then, don't tell us,
But be sure we will come to the cave. (Noh, p. 80)

A literal translation of the original corresponding to these six lines reads:

Please show us the way there.
Whom could we ask where the dew is?
Yet we wish to know where the jewel of Truth is.

In this case, Pound has added the last four lines, but at the same time, he omits the last line of the original, which refers to "the jewel of Truth" in

Buddhism. The second example is in the first speech of the old man in Part II, where Pound's translation shows only an imperfect grasp of the religious significance of the original text. Pound's version reads:

> It is a good service you have done, sir,
> A service that spreads in two worlds,
> And binds up an ancient love
> That was stretched out between them.
> I had watched for a thousand days.
> I give you largess,
> For this meeting is under a difficult law.
> (Noh, p. 82)

A more literal translation reads:

> *It is a good service you have done, sir.*
> Though three years have already gone,
> The marriage vow has not been said.
> The union of a man and a woman in love
> Is as hard as the meeting with the Buddhist law.
> (Italics indicate the part which agrees with Pound's translation.)

Thirdly, in translating the twelfth speech of the old man and sixth chorus of Part II, Pound leaves out an explicit reference to the Buddhist scripture of the original. Pound's version reads:

> The Old Man: Even to-day the difficulty of our
>   meeting is remembered,
>   And is remembered in song.
> Chorus: That we may acquire power
>   Even in our faint substance.
>   We will show forth even now,
>   And though it be but in a dream,
>   Our form of repentance. (Noh, p. 85)

A more literal translation reads:

> The Old Man: However, this day,
>   Through the rare destiny [of meeting the
>   priest]
> Chorus: We might receive the grace
>   Of the blessed scripture by our repentance.
>   Even in the dream their wish is serious.

Although some passages of Pound's *Nishikigi* may be inadequate as a translation because they are not literally faithful to the original, most of them

present the spirit and feelings of the original.
Further, except for his inadequate handling of
religious references at three places, Pound's version
is an admirable work of art, with only a few minor
flaws. There are several passages[9] in which Pound's
translation succeeds in reproducing the original text
in both the matter and the manner, as in the second
chorus of Part I:

> At last they forget, they forget,
> The wands are no longer offered,
> The custom is faded away.
> The narrow cloth of Kefu [Kyo]
> Will not meet over the breast.
> 'Tis the story of Hosonuno,
> This is the tale:
> These bodies, having no weft,
> Even now are not come together.
> Truly a shameful story.
>
> A tale to bring shame on the gods.
> Names of love,
> Now for a little spell,
> For a faint charm only,
> For a charm as slight as the binding together
> Of pine-flakes in Iwashiro,
> And for saying a wish over them about sunset,
> We return, and return to our lodging.
> The evening sun leaves a shadow. (<u>Noh</u>, p. 79)

With the exceptions of the first three lines, which do
not present the original as faithfully as the rest of
the passage, and of the eleventh line, which is an
unnecessary addition, this chorus is an excellent
translation of the original; it includes all the images
and metaphors of the original, and in my opinion, it
represents the lyricism of the original verse.

(4) AOI NO UE

The play is based on Book 9, "Aoi no Ue," of the Tale of the Genji. The story of the play is as follows. Aoi no Ue is very ill, apparently possessed by some evil spirit. Efforts to cure her have been in vain. Then a witch (Tsure; Teruhi no miko) is called in and asked to find out by her craft who or what the evil spirit is. When the witch begins to chant her spells, Shite (the spirit of Rokujo) appears and through her complaints shows the deep-rooted hatred she has for Aoi no Ue. Because Rokujo is disappointed, distressed, envious and jealous, she strikes Aoi no Ue and disappears. Then Waki (an exorcist named Yokawa no Kohijiri) appears at the request of the court to cure Aoi no Ue. The exorcist begins his powerful prayer, causing the spirit of Rokujo to reappear in the form of a female demon. Now the contest between the exorcist and Rokujo begins. The exorcist finally wins by reciting the Buddhist scripture called Hannya Kyo, which frightens Rokujo away. The play ends with the praise of the efficacy of reciting the Buddhist scripture.

The subject matter of the play is the love and jealousy of a lady of noble birth. It is important to note that although the title of the play is "Aoi no Ue," Aoi no Ue herself does not really appear in the play. She is symbolized by a sleeve on the stage. Instead, the chief character of the play, or the Shite, is the phantom of Rokujo. At the end the jealousy and anger of the spirit of Rokujo are defeated by the exorcist's recitation of the Buddhist prayers.

Ezra Pound's note given at the beginning of the two plays, Aoi no Ue and Kakitsubata, reads as follows:

> I give the next two plays, Awoi no Uye [sic] and Kakitsubata [sic], with very considerable diffidence. I am not sure that they are clear; Japanese with whom I have discussed them do not seem able to give me much help. Several passages which are, however, quite lucid in themselves, seem to me as beautiful as anything I have found in Fenollosa's Japanese notes, and these passages must be my justification. In each case I give an explanation of the story so far as I understand it. In one place I have

> transferred a refrain or doubled it. For the
> rest the plays are as literal as the notes
> before me permit. (Noh, p. 113)

I have not been able to find out with whom Pound consulted. It is unfortunate that he could not find an able person to clarify the ambiguities he found in the Fenollosa notes, for the ambiguities could have been easily resolved if Pound had asked someone who could read the original play. In this respect, I agree with Professor Arthur Waley, who comments as follows:

> There is nothing obscure or ambiguous
> in the situation. Fenollosa seems to have
> misunderstood the play and read into it
> complications and confusions which do not
> exist. He also changes the sex of the Witch
> [in Pound's version, "Miko"] though the
> Japanese word, miko, always has a feminine
> meaning.[10] (Waley, p. 180)

The most serious problem with Pound's version of Aoi no Ue is the fact that he completely misunderstands the play--he fails to realize that the title of the play does not represent its chief character--and believes that the play is a drama of the passions which torment Aoi no Ue, and that Princess Rokujo is actually Aoi no Ue in disguise. Pound fails to see that the subject matter of the play is the jealousy of Princess Rokujo which causes the illness of Aoi no Ue. This misunderstanding accounts for some passages and some remarks in Pound's version which are inaccurate or completely erroneous.[11]

Pound's "Introduction" to Aoi no Ue reveals some of his misunderstandings of the play. The introduction begins with this:

> The story, as I understand it, is that the
> "Court Lady Awoi" (Flower of the East) is
> jealous of the other and later co-wives of
> Genji. This jealousy reaches its climax, and
> she goes off her head with it, when her
> carriage is overturned and broken at the Kami
> [Kamo] festival. The play opens with the
> death-bed of Awoi. . . . (Noh, p. 113)

As the original makes clear, it is not Aoi no Ue but Princess Rokujo who is jealous.[12] Pound, however, not understanding this point, goes on to say:

> The ambiguities of certain early parts
> of the play seem mainly due to the fact that
> the "Princess Rokujo," the concrete figure on
> the stage, is a phantom or image of Awoi no
> Uye's own jealousy. That is to say, Awoi is
> tormented by her own passion, and this
> passion obsesses her first in the form of a
> personal apparition of Rukujo, then in
> demonic form. (Noh, p. 114)

Again it is not Aoi's own passion of jealousy that torments her but the jealousy of Princess Rokujo. Unaware of his misinterpretation, Pound continues his remarks:

> This play was written before Ibsen
> declared that life is a "contest with the
> phantoms of the mind." The difficulties of
> the translator have lain in separating what
> belongs to Awoi herself from the things
> belonging to the ghost of Rokujo, very much
> as modern psychologists might have difficulty
> in detaching the personality or memories of
> an obsessed person from the personal memories
> of the obsession. . . .(Noh, p. 114)

The kind of drama that Pound finds in the play--the drama within Aoi no Ue, the drama of her passion--does not exist if the play is properly understood. The action is really much simpler than Pound imagines.

Pound's introduction makes it clear that the Fenollosa manuscripts point out an important fact of the play: although the title bears her name, Aoi does not appear on the stage, but is symbolized by a folded sleeve. Pound writes:

> The Fenollosa-Hirata draft calls the
> manifest spirit "The Princess Rokujo," and
> she attacks Awoi, who is represented by the
> folded kimono [more accurately, the sleeve].
> (Noh, p. 115)

However, it seems that this explanation was not appealing or convincing to Pound, who goes on to say:

> Other texts seem to call this manifestation
> "Awoi no Uye," i.e. her mind or troubled
> spirit, and this spirit attacks her body. It

> will be perhaps simpler for the reader if I
> mark her speeches simply "Apparition," and
> those of the second form "Hannya."
> (<u>Noh</u>, p. 115)

However, not one of the texts compiled by the five schools of Noh calls the spirit "Aoi no Ue." And one cannot help wondering what "other texts" Pound consulted. In spite of the Fenollosa-Hirata draft which gives the correct interpretation of the play as Rokujo's spirit attacking Aoi's body, he confirms his point by saying:

> I do not know whether I can make the
> matter more plain or summarize it otherwise
> than by saying that the whole play is a
> dramatization, or externalization, of Awoi's
> jealousy. The passion makes her subject to
> the demon-possession. . . .(<u>Noh</u>, p. 115)

It is in the Introduction that Pound most conspicuously reveals his misinterpretation of the subject matter of the play. In his translation of the play itself, the greatest problem[13] is his handling of some of the parts which have religious references. For example, in the first speech of "Daijin,"[14] Pound's version has this sentence: "I am sent to Miko, the wise, to bid her pray to spirits." (<u>Noh</u>, p. 116).[15] The original is more explicit than Pound's "to bid her pray to spirits." The original reads: "to bid her pluck her bow-string to <u>make visible an evil spirit and tell if it be the spirit of a living man or a dead</u>." (Italics indicate the part that agrees with Waley's version.)

When the witch appears, she chants first the words of purification and then a song to invoke a spirit. Pound's version of this part is incomplete and faulty:

> Tenshojo, chishojo,
> Naigeshojo, Rakkonshojo.[16]
>
> Earth, pure earth,
> Wither, by the sixteen roots
> (Wither this evil)! (<u>Noh</u>, p. 116)

The first two lines are the transliteration of the original Japanese. The last three lines seem to be an imperfect translation of the first two lines.[17] Pound leaves out the song of invocation. A literal translation of the purification and the song may be given here:

> Pure be heaven; pure be earth.
> Pure be within and without.
> Pure be my six roots of perception.
> The spirit
> Now approaches
> At the shore of Nagahama,
> Holding loose the reins
> On the gray horse.

Pound's version of the first speech of the spirit of Rokujo (whom Pound calls the "Apparition"), who appears, invoked by the witch, begins like this:

> It may be, it may be, I come from the gate of hell in three coaches. I am sorry for Yugawo and the carriage with broken wheels. And the world is ploughed with sorrow as a field is furrowed with oxen. Man's life is a wheel on the axle, there is no turn whereby to escape. . . .
> (<u>Noh</u>, p. 116)

Concerning the opening sentence, Pound makes the following remark in the Introduction:

> The ambiguity of the apparition's opening line is, possibly, to arouse the curiosity of the audience. There will be an air of mystery, and they will not know whether it is to be the chariot associated with Genji's liaison with Yugawo, the beautiful heroine of the play Hajitomi, or whether it is the symbolic chariot drawn by a sheep, a deer, and an ox. But I think we are nearer the mark if we take Rokujo's enigmatic line, "I am come in three chariots," to mean that the formed idea of a chariot is derived from these events and from the mishap to Awoi's own chariot, all of which have combined and helped the spirit world to manifest itself concretely. (<u>Noh</u>, pp. 114-115)

"I come from the gate of hell in three coaches" (Pound's own quotation, "I am come in three chariots," is not in his version of the play) is based on a Buddhist parable in the Hokkekyo scripture. The parable tells of children who were in a burning house, but, without knowing the danger of a fire, would not leave, until their father told them that there were three coaches outside the gate, drawn, respectively, by a sheep, a deer, and an ox. Hearing these words, the children rushed out of the house, and were thus saved. In this parable, the three coaches stand for the Law of Buddhism, which leads the wandering and the ignorant of this world to enlightenment and salvation. Thus, in her opening sentence, the spirit of Rokujo wonders if her soul was able to leave this world and to attain salvation by the three coaches of the parable. Pound's "I come from the gate of hell in three coaches" is incorrect. The original, corresponding to the first sentence of Pound's version, reads:

> Could it be
> That I come out of the gate of <u>the Burning House</u>
> <u>In the three coaches</u>
> <u>That travel on the Road of Law</u>? (Italics indicate parts that agree with Waley's version.)

Instead of "the gate of hell," the original has "the gate of the Burning House," which signifies this world. Therefore, the latter of Pound's speculations, that is, "it is the symbolic chariot drawn by a sheep, a deer, and an ox," is the correct one. What he says in the last part of the quoted passage also has some truth in it, although he misunderstands the relationship between Aoi no Ue and Rokujo. The idea of a chariot seems to have a special significance to Rokujo's mind, as Waley says: "Owing to the episode at the Kamo Festival, Rokujo is obsessed by the idea of 'carriages,' 'wheels' and the like" (Waley, p. 182, n.1). But, the problem here is the fact that Pound does not seem to understand precisely the religious significance of the first sentence of Rokujo's speech, as indicated by his misinterpretation of "the gate of hell" for "the Burning House."

In the original, the second sentence of the spirit of Rokujo (which Pound translated as "I am sorry for Yugawo and the carriage with broken wheels") reads:

> My sorrow is beyond measure,
> For there is no way to drive a broken carriage
> [Which stood] at Yugao's dwelling
> [With a moonflower ("yugao") creeping on it.]

Here the playwright makes an intricate use of the word "yugao." Yugao, of course, is the name of a beautiful woman (in Book 4 of the Tale of Genji) living in obscurity and poverty with whom Genji fell in love. She died a sudden, violent death, apparently possessed or stricken by some evil spirit, in a deserted mansion where Genji took her almost by force. But "yugao" is also the name of a flower, "moonflower," creeping on the desolate mansion (where Yugao the woman died), which somehow resembles the broken carriage. Pound's "I am sorry for Yugawo . . ." is inappropriate because the speaker, the spirit of Rokujo is here referring to her own sorrow, and not concerned with Yugao. The significance of this passage is that the spirit of Rokujo soon realizes that she (or her soul) is not on the three coaches but on a broken carriage (which stands for her passions of hatred and anger), and thus far from being saved. However, Pound again fails to understand the meaning.

The third sentence in Pound's version is not quite satisfactory: "And the world is ploughed with sorrow as a field is furrowed with oxen," compared to the original:

> Sorrow of _this world_
> Is like _the wheels of the ox-cart_—
> _Round and round_ it comes.
> Is it my punishment?   (Italics indicate parts that agree with Waley's version.)

In the fourth sentence, Pound deletes a phrase taken from a Buddhist scripture. The original reads:

> Man's life is a wheel on the axle,
> There is no turn whereby to escape
> _From the Six Paths and Four Births._   (Italics indicate parts that agree with Waley's version.)

Pound's version does not have the last line.

In the middle of the play, Pound's translation of the exorcist's first speech reads:

> Do you call me to a fit place for a prayer?
> To the window of the nine wisdoms, to the
> cushion of the ten ranks, to a place full of
> holy waters, and where there is a clear moon?
>   (Noh, p. 119)

Compare this to a literal translation of the original:

> Who is it that seeks admittance while I am [practicing my religious devotion,] sitting before the window of the nine perceptions, on the floor of the ten meditations, complete with the sacred water of Yoga and the clear moon of the three mysteries?

But in the original, this passage is the exorcist's reply to a messenger (sent from the court) who "seeks admittance" to the room of the exorcist. The exorcist's words describe in Buddhist terms his sacred room, or more appropriately, his ascetic discipline.

Pound's translation of <u>Aoi no Ue</u> presents sufficiently the plot and most of the action of the original. And in such places as the dialogue between the witch and the spirit of Rokujo and the contest between the exorcist and Rokujo in the demonic form, Pound's version turns out to be a competent translation of the original. However, because of his imperfect knowledge of the religious significance of the play, his version loses some of the essential elements of the original. And, above all, misunderstanding the subject matter of the play, he was led into misinterpreting the play as a whole.

(5) KINUTA

"Kinuta" is a board over which a cloth is spread and beaten with a mallet so as to make the cloth softer. Pound's version calls it "the silk-board." The story of the play is as follows. The Waki (the husband) is absent from home for three years because of his litigations in the capital city. He sends Tsure (a maid-servant named Yugiri) to his wife (Shite), who has been left alone all these years, to tell her that he will be back by the end of the year at the latest. At home, the wife is unhappy for she is virtually deserted. When Yugiri arrives at the wife's home, the wife expresses her sorrow for being separated from her husband so long. Soon she decides to beat the silk-board (kinuta) to let out the mixed feeling of love and resentment toward her husband. Then another messenger arrives from the city, sent by the husband, conveying the message that his return will be again delayed. Angry and bitterly disappointed, the wife dies. After her death, the husband returns. Then the spirit of the wife appears, tormented and tortured because of her former resentment for her husband. Even after death, she still has a mixed feeling of love and hatred for her husband. Finally, however, she attains peace through Hokkekyo scripture, and the play ends.

The subject matter of the play is the love and resentment of a deserted wife for her husband. She beats the silk-board, letting out her longing and love for him. The title of the play, "the silk-board," is appropriate, for the wife commits all of her feelings to the board.

Pound's version of Kinuta is far more thorough and complete than his version of Aoi no Ue, Sotoba Komachi and Kayoi Komachi, although it is not free from errors and misinterpretations. Some errors are only phrasal and of minor importance to the entire play. For example,[18] in Pound's version, the opening sentence of the first speech of the husband reads: "I am of Ashiya of Kinshu, unknown and of no repute" (Noh, p. 89). The phrase, "unknown and of no repute," is an incorrect translation of the Japanese word, "nanigashi," in the original, which literally means "Mr. So-and-so." The word is used when a playwright prefers not to give a specific name to a character. Thus, "Mr. So-and-so" does not mean that the man is "unknown and of no repute," but it is a generic name given, in this play, to a considerable landlord of Ashiya of Kyushu (Pound's "Kinshu" is an error).

In some cases, by translating every word or phrase of the original Japanese literally, Pound fails to present the meaning of the original text accurately, because a literal translation sometimes gives more importance to a certain phrase than it deserves, and thus that phrase is inadequately emphasized in the translation. One example[19] is in the first part of the first chorus:

> As the decline of autumn
> In a country dwelling,
> With the grasses failing and fading--
> As men's eyes fail--
> As men's eyes fail,
> Love has utterly ceased. (Noh, p. 91)

Lines 4-5 are our concern. It is true that the original text has the word "hitome," the literal meaning of which is "men's eyes" but which means in this context something like "visitors." Thus, "As men's eyes fail" is an incorrect translation. Moreover, the original uses the word "hitome" only once; whereas Pound's version repeats "As men's eyes fail" twice, thus giving a far greater emphasis to the incorrectly rendered line.

The last part of the wife's fifth speech in Pound's version reads:

> . . . Yet I have stretched my board with patterned cloths, which curious birds brought through the twilit utter solitude, and hoped with such that I might ease my heart.
> (Noh, p. 91)

In this passage, it is unclear how Fenollosa and Pound came to translate the Japanese phrase, "totemo sabishiki kurehadori," as "which curious birds brought through the twilit utter solitude." The syllables "dori" of "kurehadori" resemble in sound a Japanese word for "birds" (when it is used as the second element of a compound word). But "kurehadori" has nothing to do with "birds"; much less with "curious birds"; it means "a weaver from Korea: or "a Korean weaver." The phrase "totemo sabishiki" means "being exceedingly lonely" or "being lonesome to death." Thus, Pound's "utter solitude" does not seem to be as removed from the original as his "curious birds" is removed from "kurehadori." The original reads: "I am lonesome to death this evening. I will beat the patterned cloth woven by a Korean weaver on the silk-board and comfort my lonely heart."

In a more or less similar manner, in translating the fifth speech of the maid-servant, which immediately follows the wife's speech discussed above, Pound changes the original. His version reads: "Boards are rough work, hard even for the poor, and you of high rank have done this to ease your heart! Here, let me arrange them, I am better fit for such business" (<u>Noh</u>, p. 92). A literal translation of the same reads: "Alas! Beating the silk-board is for the lowly. But if it is to comfort your heart, I will get it ready for you." In the original there is no word for "rough work" or "hard." Neither does the original have "and you of high rank have done this," which apparently was added by Fenollosa or Pound. Also "I am better fit for such business" is an addition to the original.[20]

So far we have discussed some of the mistranslations, which do not essentially affect the play. Next, let us consider some of those which are more serious. Earlier in the play, when the maid-servant arrives at the wife's lonely residence, the wife sadly reproaches the maid for not having sent any message to her mistress for three years while she was serving the husband. Pound's translation of the maid-servant's reply reads: "Truly I wished to come, but his Honour gave me no leisure. For three years he kept me in that very ancient city" (<u>Noh,</u> p. 90). The first sentence of Pound's translation is adequate. But the last sentence in the original reads: "For three years I stayed in the capital against my heart." Pound should have translated the last three words, "against my heart," faithfully (although the rest of the speech implies that the maid was forced to stay in the city by her master), because the phrase has a dramatic effect--it evokes an emotion and a subsequent reflection in the wife, who says (immediately after the maid's speech), echoing the maid's last words:

> You say it was against your heart
> To stay in the capital city?
> Just think, even in the city
> In the season of its blossom,
> When it abounds with delights of all sorts,
> Man's heart is not free from sorrow.

Compare this to Pound's version: "You say it was against your heart to stay in the city? While even in the time of delights I thought of its blossom, until sorrow had grown the cloak of my heart" (Noh, p. 90). It is true that Pound does present the first sentence literally, but his version does not have the same meaning or effect the original has. The second sentence is a misinterpretation. In the original, the wife, at this point, perceives the existence of sorrow even in the midst of delights.

In several places Pound fails to present the thoughts and feelings of the wife properly. For example, in the middle part of the play, the wife decides to beat the silk-board to comfort her sorrowful heart. Her action is accompanied by the following dialogue between her and the maid-servant:

Wife: I will beat the silk-board on this bed
 Which I shared with my husband.
Maid: Tears fall on the spread mat.
Wife: This will speak my sad heart.
Maid: Yugiri goes to her mistress,
Wife: And they both beat out their resentment.

The corresponding passage is translated by Pound as follows:

Wife: Beat then. Beat out our resentment.
Maid-servant: It's a coarse mat; we can never be sure. (Noh, p. 92)

Pound's version of the wife's speech gives only a half of the original, and leaves out the fact that the wife beats the silk-board on the bed on which she and her husband used to sleep--an important scene as an illustration of the wife's deep feelings toward her husband. Pound's version of the maid-servant, which makes hardly any sense, does not correspond to the original.

Again, in the wife's twelfth speech, Pound translates the last part like this: ". . . love thin as a summer cloth! Let my lord's life be even so slight, for I have no sleep under the moon. O let me go on with my cloths!" (Noh, pp. 93-94). The original reads:

57

> Love thin <u>as a summer cloth</u>--
> How loathsome!
> Yet, <u>let my lord's life be</u> long.
> Though <u>I have no sleep under the moon.</u>
> Oh, let me beat my cloths! (Italics indicate the parts which agree with Pound's translation.)

In the original, the wife refrains from wishing her husband ill, in spite of her deep grief. Pound's version, on the other hand, gives the reader an opposite impression, for Pound has the wife say, "Let my lord's life be even so slight, for I have no sleep under the moon."[21]

As in the case of <u>Sotoba Komach</u> and <u>Kayoi Komachi</u>, <u>Kinuta</u> shows an inadequate handling of the Buddhist references which are explicit in the original, particularly toward the end of the play. In the original, the first speech of the ghost of the wife[22] reads:

> Miserable is the end of my life;
> Formless, I have sunk into the hell's river of three currents.
> The light of the plum-blossoms to mark the grave
> Reveals the spring in the world of the living,
> And the kindling flame of the candle
> To light the track for the dead
> Shows the way toward the absolute Truth,
> Like the autumn moon.

The corresponding part is translated by Pound as follows:

> Ghost of the Wife: Aoi![23] for fate, fading, alas, and unformed, all sunk into the river of three currents, gone from the light of the plum flowers that reveal spring in the world!
> Chorus: She has but kindling flame to light her track. . .
> Ghost of the Wife: . . . and show her autumns of a lasting moon. . . .
> (<u>Noh</u>, p. 95)

Pound changes the original form and has the chorus interrupt the ghost of the wife. A greater problem, however, is his failure to present the clear and explicit explanation in the original of the plum-blossoms and the candle light in Buddhist terms.

The play ends with the chorus explaining how the ghost of the wife attained Buddhahood. Pound's version of the final chorus reads:

> She recites the Flower of Law; and ghost is received into Butsu; the road has become enlightened. Her constant beating of silk has opened the flower, even so lightly she has entered the seed-pod of Butsu.
> (Noh, p. 97)

It is not "She [the ghost of the wife]" but the husband who recites the scripture. Pound apparently is unaware that before the final chorus, the husband, seeing the ghost of his wife approach, prays, reciting the Hokkekyo scripture ("the Flower of Law") with his prayer beads in his hands. Thus, the original ends with the following speech of the chorus:

> The recitation of the scripture Hokkekyo
> Cleared the way for the ghost toward salvation.
> This was possible because
> Her beating of the silk-board for consolation
> Opened the flower of the Law
> And produced the seed of Buddhahood.

"Her constant beating of silk has opened the flower" in Pound's version is not as explicit as the original in presenting why the ghost of the wife could attain Buddhahood.

Despite such weaknesses as the imperfect understanding of the wife's character (her way of thinking and the depth of her feelings), the inadequate treatment of religious references, and the faulty ending, in some parts of Kinuta, Pound shows his excellence as a poet-translator. For example, he translates the wife's first speech as follows:

> Sorrow!--
> Sorrow is in the twigs of the duck's nest
> And in the pillow of the fishes,
> At being held apart in the waves,
> Sorrow between mandarin ducks,
> Who have been in love
> Since time out of mind.
> Sorrow--
> There is more sorrow between the united
> Though they move in the one same world.
> O low 'Remembering-grass',

> I do not forget to weep
> At the sound of the rain upon you,
> My tears are a rain in the silence,
> O heart of the seldom clearing. (<u>Noh</u>, p. 90)

In the original the passage is also written in verse and expresses the deep-felt sorrow of the wife who is kept apart from her husband. Strictly speaking, lines 5-8 of Pound's version have no exact correspondence to the original; they are an amplification of the original, most of which is represented by Pound's second line, "Sorrow is in the twigs of the duck's nest." I believe, however, this addition by Pound is an improvement, rather than a defect, for it strengthens the feeling of the original. Not only the feeling but all the images, metaphors and analogies of the original--"the twigs of the duck's nest," "the pillow of the fishes," and the analogy between the wife's sorrowful heart with the external world of nature--are skillfully rendered into moving poetry. The use of the antonyms of the original is also successfully reproduced in the last five lines: "to remember" in the "low 'remembering-grass'" and "to forget" in "I do not forget to weep"; and the "rain" and the "clearing" in the last two lines.

Pound's translation of the thirteenth chorus is another example of a successful presentation of the original--its contents, words and images accurately and adequately rendered--probably with two exceptions: in line 9, some may question the effectiveness and appropriateness of Pound's use of "Aoi! Aoi!"[24] in place of "Oh, horror!"; in line 10, the original uses "sheep," which Pound translates as "sleep." (This error may well be typographical.) Like the original, Pound's version in the second paragraph skillfully handles a Buddhist idea in the verse form. Pound's translation reads like this:

> Ah false desire and fate!
> Her tears are shed on the silk-board,
> Tears fall and turn into flame,
> The smoke has stifled her cries,
> She cannot reach us at all,
> Nor yet the beating of the silk-board
> Nor even the voice of the pines,
> But only the voice of that sorrowful punishment.
>   Aoi!   Aoi!
> Slow as the pace of sleep,
> Swift as the steeds of time,

By the six roads of changing and passing
We do not escape from the wheel,
Nor from the flaming of Karma,
Though we wander through life and death;
This woman fled from his horses
To a world without taste or breath. (<u>Noh</u>, p. 96)[25]

Notes to Chapter II

1. Teele, p. 170.

2. The Japanese texts used for my study are as follows: Yokyoku Shu. ed. Mario Yokomichi and Akira Omote. 2 vols. (Tokyo: Iwanami Shoten, 1960 [Vol. I], 1962 [Vol. II].)
For these six plays--Tamura, Suma Genji, Nishikigi, Choryo, Kakitsubata and Genjo--which are not included in Yokyoku Shu, I used the following texts:

Choryo. ed. Kanze Sakon. (Tokyo: Hinoki Shoten, 1966.)
Genjo. ed. Kanze Sakon. (Tokyo: Hinoki Shoten, 1966.)
Kakitsubata. ed. Kanze Sakon. (Tokyo: Hinoki Shoten, 1966.)
Nishikigi. ed. Kanze Sakon (Tokyo: Hinoki Shoten, 1966.)
Suma Genji. ed. Kanze Sakon (Tokyo: Hinoki Shoten, 1966.)
Tamura. ed. Kanze Sakon (Tokyo: Hinoki Shoten, 1966.)

3. Waley, pp. 150-160.

4. Another point we notice in Pound's translation of this play is the fact that he apparently ignores a typical technique of the Noh play--the use of an exchange of words between two or more characters. For example, in the original, the priest, seeing Komachi sitting on the sotoba, says first to himself, "Look! It is a sotoba that the beggar there is sitting on. I shall give her a lesson to come off it," and then speaks directly to Komachi: "Now, the beggar woman, there, isn't it a sotoba, an embodiment of the gracious body of Buddha, that you are sitting on? Come off it and rest somewhere else." But Pound omits the priest's address. This omission further affects the translation of Komachi's reply to the priest's remonstrance. Her reply in the original reads: "Though you said it was the gracious body of Buddha, I saw no writing on it, nor any figure carved. I thought it was merely a decayed tree." Whereas Pound's translation reads: "Eh, for all your blather it has no letters on it, not a smudge of old painting. I thought it was only a stick" (Noh, p. 13). Because Pound omitted the priest's speech explaining the "stick" on which Komachi sits as

"the gracious body of Buddha," Pound obviously should not have Komachi say, "Though you said it was the gracious body of Buddha."

   5. Among the Fenollosa manuscripts housed in Beinecke Library, there are two typed pages of the translation of <u>Sotoba Komachi</u>. Curiously enough, Ono's opening lines in Pound's version, in which "I spoke like the nightingales" appears, are not included in these two pages.

   6. There are more examples of additions for explanatory purposes. The following are some of them (all from Part I)--Italics indicate the parts added to the original:
   (1) the third speech of the priest: "Yes, I know that the cloth of this place and the lacquers are famous things. <u>I have already heard of their glory</u>, and yet I still wonder why they have such great reputation" (<u>Noh</u>, p. 77).
   (2) the second speech of the old woman: "Well now, that's a disappointment. Here they call the wood 'Nishikigi,' and the woven stuff 'Hosonuno,' and yet you come saying that you have never heard why, <u>and never heard the story</u>. Is it reasonable?" (<u>Noh</u>, p. 78)
   (3) the third speech of the old woman:
   <u>These names are surely a byword</u>.
   As the cloth Hosonuno is narrow of weft.
   More narrow than the breast,
   We call by this name any woman
   Whose breasts are hard to come nigh to.
   <u>It is a name in the books of love</u>. (<u>Noh</u>, p. 78)

   7. Another example of amplification is in the fifth speech of the old woman. The original reads: "and the sound of the autumn insects," compared to Pound's version: "It was a sweet sound like katydids and crickets./A thin sound like the Autumn" (<u>Noh</u>, p. 84).

   8. This line is an incorrect translation of the original, which reads: "Where the leaves have changed colors."

   9. Lines 7-11 of the fourth chorus of Part I; lines 6-10, 13-16 of the sixth chorus of Part II, in addition to the one discussed above.

   10. See Note 14 below.

11. For example, in his note to the third speech of the spirit of Rokujo, Pound misinterprets the apparition of Rokujo as an evil spirit of Aoi no Ue. Again in his translation of the second chorus, he does not make clear the relationship of Aoi and Rokujo to Hikaru Genji.

12. In modern psychology, Aoi's illness may be diagnosed as a result of her frustration and jealousy, but in the Tale of Genji, the popular belief of the period--that the "evil" spirit of one who is jealous of someone else can possess the object of one's jealousy-- is presented.

13. Another, less serious, problem is found in the third speech of the spirit of Rokujo, in which she tells briefly of her past life, alluding to the episodes in the "Book of Aoi" of the Tale of Genji (on which the entire play is based). Pound's version of this passage shows that he is not sufficiently acquainted with the source, the "Book of Aoi." Had he been more familiar with it, he could have reduced the number of inaccuracies and misinterpretations in his translation of the passage.

14. The term "Daijin," used in Pound's version, is inaccurate. The original identifies this character as "Ason" or a courtier.

15. In the First and Second printings of the New Directions paperback edition of the text, there is an error in this sentence, identifying the Miko as male, so that the line reads: "I am sent to Miko, the wise, to bid him pray to spirits" (Noh, p. 116). The Fourth and subsequent printings corrected the error. The Third printing is not available for checking.

16. "Rakkonshojo" is an error for "Rokkonshojo."

17. If Pound meant the last two lines to be the translation of the first two, "the sixteen roots" of line 4 is an error for "the six roots." And the original has no words for "Wither" (line 4) or "(Wither this evil)!" (line 5).

18. Another example is the phrase, "this side," in the wife's second speech: "What! you say it is Yugiri? There is no need for a servant. Come to this side! in here!" (Noh, p. 90). "This side" is an

inadequate translation of the Japanese word, "konata," which could mean, in some other contexts, "this side," but which should be translated as "here" in this context. Pound (or Fenollosa) translated the word "konata" as "this side" again in the speech of the angel in Hagoromo (Noh, p. 99), where it means "me." In the priest's second speech in Kumasaka, however, the same word is correctly translated as "me" (Noh, p. 39). Therefore, it is hard to tell whether or not Fenollosa or Pound knew precisely how the word "konata" should be translated in different contexts.

19. Again, in the ninth speech of the chorus, line 3, "So thin are the summer cloths!", is in my opinion an unnecessary addition. Although the word "cloths" does appear in the original, it is hardly worth translating the word literally in this case. In fact, sometimes a certain word is used in the original almost without any meaning, except for its effect as a pun. And the word "cloths" is used for such purpose. Therefore, to make a full line for this word is to give more importance to the word than it really deserves. For this reason line 3 should be omitted.

20. We may add, however, that this passage is less objectionable than the other in that Pound has not really changed the sense of the original text.

21. There is another example of a similar distortion of the original. Pound's version of the last three lines of the ninth chorus reads:

As a floating shadow of the water grass,
That the ripples break on the shore?
O foam, let him be as brief. (Noh, p. 94)

According to this translation, it sounds as if the wife wishes her husband's life to be short--or, another interpretation may be also possible: she wishes his stay in the city be as brief as possible. However, the original which is rather difficult to translate into English means neither one nor the other. Instead, the original says something to this effect: "Would that the lovers could be brought together, like the foams brought to the shore by the ripples and waves."

22. In the play, the wife dies of grief when she receives the message that her husband's return will be delayed again. When the husband does return, the wife appears as a ghost.

23. In translating <u>Kinuta</u> Pound uses an expression "Aoi!" six times: at the beginning of the twelfth speech of the wife, and of the first speech of the ghost of the wife; twice in the middle of the thirteenth chorus; and twice toward the end of the fourteenth chorus. The same expression is found in Pound's <u>Cantos</u>. It seems that Pound intends to impart some emotional quality by using the expression "Aoi!", although it is not clear what kind of emotion is meant. The <u>Annotated Index to the Cantos</u> gives the following information: "'Aoi': an expression of uncertain meaning; it occurs 172 times in the Oxford manuscript of the <u>Chanson de Roland</u>, generally following the last line of a <u>laisse</u>. . . " [John Hamilton Edwards, <u>et al</u>., <u>Annotated Index to the Cantos of Ezra Pound</u> (Berkeley and Los Angeles: University of California Press, [1957], 1971), p. 10].

24. For the comment on this expression, see Footnote 22 above.

25. As a third example of an excellent translation, we may quote the fifth chorus:

> The stag's voice has bent her heart toward sorrow,
> Sending the evening winds which she does not see,
> We cannot see the tip of the branch.
> The last leaf falls without witness.
> There is an awe in the shadow,
> And even the moon is quiet,
> With the love-grass under the eaves.
> (<u>Noh</u>, pp. 92-93).

CHAPTER III

EZRA POUND'S TRANSLATIONS

OF ELEVEN MORE NOH PLAYS

In Chapter II we discussed the major problems and characteristics presented in Pound's translations of the four plays. In this chapter we shall consider the quality of the rest of his translations chiefly in relation to what we have discovered in the previous chapter. Of the eleven plays, <u>Kayoi Komachi</u> is given a more detailed discussion than the rest, so that it may also serve as a general reference.

KAYOI KOMACHI

Like <u>Sotoba Komachi</u>, this play is based on the legend of Ono no Komachi. The title means "Coming to Komachi." "Kayoi" means "coming" or "going" continuously. The chief character of this play, however, is not Ono but Shosho. The first part of the play is a dialogue between the Waki (a priest) and the Tsure (Ono no Komachi as a shabby old woman), a dialogue which reveals Ono living an obscure life. When the priest asks who she is, she disappears, ashamed of her present situation, hinting vaguely that she is Ono no Komachi, living in Ichiwarano. The priest guesses who she is, and decides to go there and pray for her spirit. When the priest says the prayer in Ichiwarano, Ono, this time as a beautiful young woman, reappears and expresses her joy over the prospect of attaining Buddhahood through the prayer. Hearing this, the Shite (Shosho), who has appeared on the stage during the priest's prayer, tries to dissuade her from accepting the prayer. Shosho expresses his strong love and desire for Ono. Now the priest knows who the man and the woman really are, and tries to persuade both of them to accept the prayer so as to be saved. Shosho and Ono tell the story of Shosho who as an unsuccessful suitor came to Ono for ninety-nine nights. At the end of the play, the chorus tells us that Ono and Shosho both attained peace and Buddhahood--Ono, because of her constant wish for salvation; and Shosho, because of his "one act of discipline."

The major interest of the play is in the intensity of young love, which remains alive even after the man or his flesh is dead. However, the play is not an exultation of such love, for it ends with the fulfillment of Ono's wish for salvation, not only for herself but for Shosho. Again, as in <u>Sotoba Komachi</u>, the religious overtone is important in the play.

Discussion of Pound's Version

One characteristic of a Noh play is its frequent use of folk legends and literary materials well-known to its audience. Sometimes a play is entirely based on a certain legend or a literary work; sometimes, a character's speeches contain allusions to famous names in literature. <u>Kayoi Komachi</u> is based on the legend of Ono no Komachi, who is known to the Japanese people as a woman of beauty and pride and as an excellent poet in her youth but who ended her life in destitution and humiliation. Thus, at her first appearance (as an old woman) in the play, the playwright purposely has her say:

'Tis a pity, indeed,
To wear clothes unperfumed
And to gather wood for fuel.

to exploit the pathos which the audience would feel, when it hears her describe her present misery and hint at her past glory. Pound's translation does not include these three lines, which are important for their emotional impact on the audience.

In her second speech Ono enumerates the various kinds of fruit she has and tells us of what some of them remind her—particularly the names of famous poets, thus indirectly referring to the fact that she herself was once a renowned poet. In this speech, again, Pound leaves out the allusions and associations to the poets which Ono makes with the names of fruit. By this omission, Pound's translation fails to give sufficiently the deep feelings which the original passage has. A comparison of Pound's version with a more literal translation may make the point clearer. Pound's translation reads: "I've nuts and kaki and chestnuts and plums and peaches, and big and little oranges, and a bunch of tachibana, which reminds me of days that are gone" (Noh, p. 16). A more literal translation reads:

> Ono: Here is a sweet acorn
> Helpless before a stormy wind,
> Resembling a carriage I used to ride.
> Chorus: The fruit in a poet's house--
> Here is a persimmon after which
> Ono: The poet Hitomaro took his name.
> This is a small chestnut,
> Reminding one of the poet Yamabe.
> Chorus: Here are plums from the window,
> Ono: And peaches from the orchard,
> Chorus: And pears from Ono-ura,
> Famous for the hemp, too.
> Also are there various nuts,
> *And big and little oranges* and kumquats,
> *And a spray of tachibana* [orange flower],
> *Which reminds me of days that are gone.*
> (Italics indicate the parts which agree with Pound's translation.)

Another weakness of Pound's translation of Kayoi Komachi is the characterization of Ono. Pound leaves out some parts pertaining to Ono's character--a description of her present condition, her awareness of the changes in her fortune, her nostalgia for the glorious past, her search for salvation through a priest's prayer. We do not know whether it is Pound or Fenollosa who deleted these parts. At any rate, Pound does not seem to understand the character of Ono in the play adequately, particularly her genuine wish for salvation through prayer. This lack of understanding seems to account for some of Pound's inaccurate or ambiguous interpretations.

One other major problem in Pound's versoin of Kayoi Komachi is the frequent omission of religious references. (We may note here that Pound's version of Sotoba Komachi, which suffers from heavy cuts, leaves out almost all the references to Buddhist doctrines contained in the original text.) An example is in his translation of Ono's first speech: "I am a woman who lives out about Itchiharano.[1] There are many rich houses in Yase, and I take fruit and wood to them, and there's where I'm going now" (Noh, p. 16). Let us compare this with a literal translation of the corresponding part in the original:

> *I am a woman who lives out about*
> Ichiwarano. Because there is a reverend person staying in the village of Yase, I come every day with fruit and wood for fuel. I have come again today. [To the priest] What shall I say? I have come again. (Italics indicate the part which agrees with Pound's translation.)

Pound's translation, "There are many rich houses in Yase," is a misinterpretation. The part should read: "Because there is a reverend person staying in Yase," referring to the priest. Again this is an important point in regard to Ono's character in this play. She wishes for her salvation through a priest's prayer. This is why she has come to the priest every day with humble presents; it is not because "There are many rich houses in Yase" where she could sell "fruit and wood" as Pound's version suggests.

A little later in the play, in translating Ono's reply to the priest, who asks her name, Pound leaves out her concern for a prayer. Pound's translation of Ono's answer reads: "(To herself.) I can't tell him that [her name] now. (To him.) I'm just a woman who lives out by Ichihara-no-be [sic], in all that wild grass there" (Noh, p. 17). In the original, the passage is divided into two parts:

> Ono: I am too ashamed of myself to tell my name.[2]
> Chorus: I cannot tell my name.
>   I am an old woman living in Ichiwarano,
>   Where grows the pampas grass.
>   Oh, Sir priest, please say a prayer for me.
>   So saying, she disappeared;
>   So saying, she disappeared.

It seems that Pound fails to understand Ono's wish for salvation through prayer—an important aspect of her character throughout the play.

Pound's translation of Ono's fourth speech is better than some other passages but not completely satisfactory. Pound's version reads: "There's a heap of good in your prayers; do you think you could bring me to Buddha?" (Noh, p. 17). Whereas the original reads: "Happy am I to hear your prayer./ I wish you would not only pray for me/ But *bring me to Buddha* by giving me Buddist precepts." (Italics indicate the part which agrees with Pound's translation.) Pound's translation, "There's a heap of good in your prayers," is extremely colloquial and such colloquialism is out of place, because it does not reproduce the proper tone of the original text which is quite formal. Pound's version of Shosho's first speech (which follows immediately Ono's fourth speech) is ambiguous: "It's an ill time to do that. Go back. You move in ill hours" (Noh, p. 17). A literal translation of the same speech is as follows: [Having heard Ono's wish to attain Buddhahood through the prayer of the priest, the spirit of Shosho says:] "I will be bitter if you accept precepts./ And you, priest, be gone." Pound's version of Ono's fifth speech, which comes immediately after Shosho's first speech, is not satisfactory. It reads: "I say they were very fine prayers. I will not come back without a struggle" (Noh, p. 17). A more literal translation reads: "Alas! Just as soon as I thought/ I could finally attain Buddhahood,/ Did you appear to show me the tortures of hell!" Pound's version does not sufficiently present Ono's strong wish for salvation.[3]

Pound's tenth chorus, which is next to the last speech of the play, is a misinterpretation. It reads: "Though she only asks me to drink a cup of moonlight, I will not take it. It is a trick to catch one for Buddha" (Noh, p. 20). In this translation it sounds as if Ono tries to play a "trick" on Shosho to convert him. In the original, however, the idea of drinking wine (which is not made clear in Pound's version) to celebrate the reunion of Shosho and Ono comes from Shosho himself; it is not suggested by Ono. The chorus speaks for Shosho:

> How about a cup of wine
> [To celebrate my reunion with Ono]?
> Even if the wine were poured
> In a cup as beautiful as the present moon,
> I should refrain,
> Since Buddha so teaches us.

After this, the original has two important lines which Pound does not present. It reads: "Because of this one act of discipline,/ His sins vanished." Pound's translation fails to show the fact that Shosho "refrained" from taking a cup of wine of his own accord, remembering Buddha's teaching, and that therefore, his sins vanished and he could attain Buddhahood. Although Pound's translation does have the final part of the play in the final chorus, which reads: "Both their sins vanished. They both became pupils of Buddha, both Komachi and Shosho" (<u>Noh</u>, p. 21), Pound does not seem to understand why both Ono and Shosho could attain Buddhahood, for he gives the following comment at the end of the play: "This eclogue is very incomplete. Ono seems rather like Echo, and without the last two lines of the chorus one could very well imagine her keeping up her tenzone with Shosho until the end of time" (<u>Noh</u>, p. 21). One may suspect that it was not Pound that deleted the sentence, "Because of this one act of discipline,/ His sins vanished," but that he did not find it in the Fenollosa manuscripts.[4] Had Pound seen the sentence, or had he known it, which explains the reason for Shosho's attainment of Buddhahood, Pound would have better understood why Ono and Shosho finally attained peace and salvation. Pound's final comment also indicates the fact that he fails to understand Ono's basic character in this play and her genuine wish for salvation.

Pound's version of <u>Kayoi Komachi</u>--although it is more complete than <u>Sotoba Komachi</u> and has some passages skillfully translated[5]--does not sufficiently represent the most essential quality of the original play, because Pound only imperfectly grasped the religious significance and the character of Ono, the latter of which cannot be fully appreciated without the knowledge of the folk legend and literary materials pertaining to her life; and Pound apparently did not have this knowledge.

TAMURA

The play is about a historical figure, Sakanoue no Tamura Maro (a great war-general; 758-811). The story is as follows: the Waki (a priest from the eastern part of Japan) has come to Kiyomizu Temple in Kyoto. It is March and the cherry-blossoms are in full bloom. The priest watches them. There comes a boy with a broom and sweeps the ground underneath the cherry-tree. The priest asks the boy about the tradition and legend of the temple. The boy tells the priest that the temple was built by Kenshin under the patronage of Sakanoue no Tamura Maro. The boy also explains about the famous temples nearby. After the sunset, the moonlight shines on the cherry-blossoms. The boy and the priest admire the scene and also praise Kannon (the Buddhist goddess of mercy). Struck with something uncommon about the boy, the priest asks who he is. The boy answers: "If you want to know who I am, look where I am going." So saying, the boy enters the chapel called Tamura-do (a chapel in commemoration of Tamura). The boy is the ghost of Sakanoue no Tamura Maro in disguise. After this, while the priest recites the Hokkekyo scripture, Sakanoue no Tamura Maro appears and tells a story of his conquest of the devil in Mt. Suzuka with the protection of Kannon. The play ends with the end of the story. The subject matter of the play is Tamura's victory in a battle and his strong faith in Kannon. The war and religion are thematically combined in this play.

Pound's translation of Tamura has problems similar to those we find in his version of Sotoba Komachi. Pound remarks at the beginning of the play: "The notes [the Fenollosa manuscripts] are in fragments, or rather there are several long cuts, which do not, however, obscure the outline or structure of the play" (Noh, p. 49). The beginning part of the play (of thirty lines) is omitted, although Pound gives a summary of the opening--the time is spring; cherry-blossoms are blooming; the setting is the Kiyomizu temple; a boy appears and praises Kannon. The second long cut occurs in the middle of the play, after the Waki's (the priest) fifth speech. Pound explains the omission of this portion (of fifteen lines) with a brief note: "There is a break here in the notes. There should follow a chorus about cherries [cherry-blossoms] under the moon" (Noh, p. 50). Pound's explanation presents only the half of the whole picture. The first half of the passage (spoken by the chorus) describes the beautiful evening scene around the temple with the cherry-blossoms in full bloom and the moon shining brightly. In the middle, the Shite (a boy) interrupts and speaks one line; then the chorus resumes the speech. The second half contains praise for the grace of Kannon which is reflected in the beautiful landscape. The third cut--shorter than the first two--is in the final chorus of the play. Pound leaves out the last part of the original text of the chorus--a quotation from the Hokkekyo scripture, commending the great power of Kannon. Thus, each of the three cuts has a specific reference to the Kannon. Since the subject matter of the play is Tamura's victory in a battle and his strong faith in Kannon, and since the grace of Kannon is said to bring about the victory and is thus thematically important, Pound's version loses some of the essential points of the play.

In translating <u>Tamura</u>, Pound sometimes condenses the original, though less frequently than in <u>Sotoba Komachi</u>. In the third chorus of Part II of <u>Tamura</u>, for example, Pound condenses the length of the original into less than half, omitting many of the details in the original, although he presents the most important point of the passage. A comparison of Pound's translation with the original shows the problem clearly. Pound's version reads:

> There the plum-trees were blossoming. All the scene showed the favour of Kwannon [Kannon] and the virtue of the Emperor.
> Then there was a great noise of evil voices, a shaking of mountains. (<u>Noh</u>, p. 52)

A more literal translation reads like this:

> Bows and horses were ready for battle.
> In every flower and leaf
> Of the plum-trees blossoming there,
> The victory seemed to be promised.
> The warrior's cast-iron heart was wholly devoted
> To the holy country of the emperor.
> Besides, the country was protected
> By the grace of Kannon,
> Who would help the soldiers in the battle.
> The evil spirits at Suzuka
> Knew nothing of this sort awaiting them.
> <u>Then there was a great noise of evil voices</u>
> Which shook the hills and dales.
> The resounding noise filled the air
> And the whole mountain was in turmoil.
> (Italics indicate the part which agrees with Pound's translation.)

Aside from the fact that the original verse form is changed into prose, the first three lines of Pound's translation are a summary of the first nine lines of the original. Pound gives the general meaning but not the manner in which the original expresses the matter. His translation ignores the careful attention the original pays to "every flower and leaf" or to the "warrior's cast-iron heart."

TSUNEMASA

The play is about the warrior, Tsunemasa, of the Taira, who fell at the battle of Ichi-no-tani in 1184. At the beginning of the play, the Waki (a priest named Gyokei) tells the final story of Tsunemasa: Tsunemasa was loved by the Emperor but was killed at the battle. Now the priest is to perform a music service in commemoration of Tsunemasa, and to dedicate to Buddha the stringed musical instrument called Seizan. (The instrument was loaned to Tsunemasa by the Emperor). Then the ghost of the Shite (Tsunemasa) appears, telling who he is. Tsunemasa, as a ghost, is still strongly attached to this world. He tells of his youthful life and how he used to play the instrument Seizan. His nostalgia for a worldly merriment is strong, but he is ashamed of his clinging to the world. After expressing his shame for exposing his worldly passions to living people, he disappears and the play ends. The play has a Buddhist theme of a dead person whose flesh left the world by death but whose spirit longs for the pleasures of this world, and who thus is deeply ashamed of himself for retaining the worldly desires after death.

In his "Foreword" to Tsunemasa Pound writes:

> The Noh, especially the Noh of spirits, abounds in dramatic situations, perhaps too subtle and fragile for our western stage, but none the less intensely dramatic. . .
>
> Tsunemasa [sic] is gentle and melancholy. It is all at high tension, but it is a psychological tension, the tension of the seance. The excitement and triumph are the nervous excitement and triumph of a successful ritual. The spirit is invoked and appears.
>
> The parallels with Western spiritist doctrines are more than interesting. Note the spirit's uncertainty as to his own success in appearing. The priest wonders if he really saw anything. The spirit affirms that 'The body was there if you saw it.' (Noh, p. 54)

On the basis of what Pound says in this foreward, particularly in the second and third paragraphs, we suspect that he misunderstands the play. His remarks suggest that the central interest of the play is in the "psychological tension" felt in the "ritual," or the "seance," which succeeds in invoking the spirit of the dead. However, the play essentially deals with the Buddhist theme of a man's spirit tormented by his inability to relinquish worldly desires even after his death. It is true that the play begins with a "ritual," but it is not the kind associated with the spiritualist's seance, the purpose of which is to "invoke" the spirit; it is a religious service, praying for the salvation of the warrior Tsunemasa, who was killed recently in battle. Concerning the third paragraph, we should quote the dialogue in which the sentence, "The body was there if you saw it," appears in Pound's translation:

> Spirit: It is there if you see it.
> Priest: I can see.
> Spirit: Are you sure that you see it, really?
> Priest: O, do I, or do I not see you?
>
> (Noh, p. 55)

Compare this to a more literal translation of the corresponding original text:

> Spirit: Now it [the ghost of Tsunemasa] is visible;
> Priest: Now it is not;
> Spirit: Whether the form is,
> Priest: Or not,
> Spirit: Is ambiguous.

The original text simply presents the fact that the ghost of Tsunemasa ("Spirit") becomes visible one moment and invisible the next. The original does not indicate, either explicitly or implicitly, "the spirit's uncertainty as to his own success in appearing." Neither is it true that "the spirit affirms that 'The body was there if you saw it.'" The quoted sentence is not in the original; it is the translator's creation, a result of reading something more than appears in the original.

In the same play, after the first speech of the priest, the original has a section (of twenty-six lines) spoken successively by the priest, chorus and Tsunemasa's ghost. Pound omits the entire portion with a brief stage direction: "They perform a service to the spirit of Tsunemasa" (Noh, p. 54). Both the priest and chorus express the meaning of the religious service performed for Tsunemasa's soul. The speech of

Tsunemasa's ghost reveals the spirit of Tsunemasa still strongly attached to the pleasures of the world. Since the play is centered around the hero, whose spirit finds it difficult to detach himself from the worldly desires after death, the omission of this section is a more serious loss than it seems in Pound's version.

In another part of the play (the second chorus through the eighth speech of the spirit of Tsunemasa in Pound's version), Pound reduces the original text of thirty lines to only seven. In this section, the original has the chorus tell of the past glory of Tsunemasa, a part which Pound omits almost entirely. This section is essential to the subject matter of the play--the characterization of Tsunemasa, whose spirit adheres to this world, despite his knowledge that his desire is shameful. The chorus' telling of Tsunemasa's glorious history indirectly accounts for his strong nostalgia for the past. Therefore, by cutting this speech Pound loses an essential part of the play.

SUMA GENJI

Like Aoi no Ue, Suma Genji is also based on the Tale of Genji by Lady Murasaki (978-1016?). Fujiwara no Okinori (the Waki, a priest) arrives at the seashore of Suma on his way to Ise Shrine. An old woodcutter appears, carrying cut-wood on his back, and stops at a cherry-tree and looks at it. Okinori asks if the tree has some significance. The old man says that it is the famous cherry-tree related to Prince Hikaru Genji, the hero of the Tale of Genji. The old man tells a life story of the prince and disappears, vaguely hinting that he is the Hikaru Genji himself. Okinori, wishing to see more of this unusual manifestation, decides to stay at the shore for a little while. Then, Prince Genji, in his bright costume, appears, telling Okinori that he descended from heaven to this shore of Suma to save the mortals. Then he dances. At dawn he disappears and the play ends. The subject matter is Hikaru Genji himself--glorification of the hero in the Tale of Genji as a god-figure descending from heaven to help the mortals.

One interesting aspect of the play is the fact that the author refers, usually quite explicitly, to various parts of the Tale of Genji throughout the play. Pound, however, does not seem to be sufficiently acquainted with the source and fails to present adequately the references to the Tale from the original. The most conspicuous example of these failures occurs in the first speech of the chorus, which narrates the life of Prince Genji and gives the titles of the books from the Tale pertaining to the hero. Pound, however, misses the point entirely and translates the titles of the books as place names. Thus, Pound's translation reads: "I was chujo[6] in Hahakigi province. I was chujo in the land of the maple-feasting. . . I was naidaijin in Miwotsukushi, I was dajodaijin in the lands of Otome, and daijotenno in Fufi no Uraba. . ." (Noh, p. 23). A correct translation should read: "I was chujo in the 'Book of Hahakigi'. I was sho sammi [instead of "chujo"] in the 'Book of the Maple-feasting' . . . I was naidaijin in the 'Book of Miwotsukushi'; dajodaijin in the 'Book of Otome'; and dajotenno [instead of "daijotenno"] in the 'Book of Fuji [instead of "Fufi"] no Uraba' . . ." The original text has another reference to the Tale of Genji in the third chorus:

> And he will descend from heaven in the moonlight
> And will appear on this sea-shore.
> So says the old man,
> And now he is gone in the clouds,
> As the title of a book in the Tale of Genji,
> The 'Book of Kumogakure' ["Getting behind the cloud"].
> He vanished, he vanished,
> Behind the cloud.

Pound's translation of the corresponding part reads: "Wait and the moon will show him./ That woodman is gone in the clouds" (Noh, p. 24). Pound's translation does not present the allusion to the Tale explicitly, although it has the line, "That woodman is gone in the clouds." Thus it is doubtful whether Pound knew of the allusion to the Tale in this sentence or not.

GENJO

The title of the play is the name of biwa, a musical instrument with four strings, brought from China and owned by Emperor Murakami (926-967). In the play, however, the name Genjo is mentioned only twice, and it is not clear (even in the original text) whether <u>Genjo</u> is brought to the stage by one of the characters or not. The story of the play is as follows: Fujiwara no Moronaga (c. 1180), the famous biwa player, stops at an old couple's house on the sea-shore of Suma, on his way to China where he intends to learn more advanced techniques of biwa playing. Moronaga plays his biwa at the request of his host and hostess, but the rain falling on the wooden eves disturbs the music. The old couple thatches the roof to muffle the rain. Moronaga is impressed with the high degree of appreciation of music the old couple shows and asks them to play some music for him. The couple begins to play. Moronaga is surprised with the divinely perfect performance of the couple and feels deeply ashamed of his pride in his skill which is less perfect and is about to leave for his home, giving up the idea of going to China. The old couple stops him and tells him that they are actually the spirits of Emperor Murakami and Lady Nashitsubo in disguise in order to dissuade Moronaga from going to China. Then the two disappear temporarily.

In Part II, the spirit of Emperor Murakami appears. He explains that of three instruments brought from China (Genjo, Seizan and Shishimaru), Shishimaru was kept by the dragon-god under the sea. The Emperor bids the dragon-god bring back Shishimaru. The order obeyed, Shishimaru is brought back to the Emperor, who gives it to Moronaga and teaches some art. Then the Emperor leaves the scene, riding the chariot drawn by the winged horses (the action is symbolically presented in the dance); Moronaga returns to his city, riding a fast horse, bearing the biwa Shishimaru with him. The play ends here.

Pound's translation of <u>Genjo</u> is a fairly satisfactory work. Probably the only serious problem is his misunderstanding of the situation in Part II. Pound assigns the entire Part II to the Emperor Murakami, whereas in the original, the Emperor, the dragon-god and the chorus participate in the dialogue.⁷ In the original, the first speaker, the Emperor, bids the dragon-god bring the stringed instrument to him, and the order is quickly obeyed. Pound's translation, however, does not present this fact. It shows that the Emperor called on the dragon-god but it fails to show why. In the middle part of the entire passage, Pound's version does not give accurately the action of the dragon-god (described in the dialogue) in relation to the musical instrument which he has brought with him. The translation indicates that Pound did not understand the situation which is clear in the original.

SHOJO

Shojo is a very short "dance" piece as Pound's introductory notes indicate:

> This little dance-plan or eclogue is, evidently, one of the 'opening or closing pieces in praise of the gods or the reign.' It is merely a little service of praise to the wine-spirit. It is quite easy to understand, from such a performance as this, why one meets travellers who say, 'Noh? I've seen Noh Dances; I know nothing about Noh Plays.'
> (Noh, p. 46)

"Shojo" is an imaginary monster of China, resembling and friendly to a human being and very fond of sake. The play has its setting in China. The story is very simple. Kofu, a Chinese sake-merchant, has become wealthy by selling sake at the market at Yang-tze. This evening, Kofu awaits Shojo, who often comes to buy sake from him. Shojo comes and praises the obedient heart of Kofu and dances a dance praising sake. Shojo's dance is the main interest of the play.

Pound's version is generally satisfactory, except for the opening part, where we find an example of condensation and an inadequate sentence identifying a shojo. A comparison of Pound's version with the original will illustrate the point:

Pound's version

Waki: . . . No matter how much he drinks, his
face shows no change. It is curious.
When I asked his name, he said, 'Shojo.'
A shojo is a monkey. I waited for him
where the river runs out at Jinyo,
clipping chrysanthemum petals into the
sake. I waited for him before moon-rise.

Chorus: This is chrysanthemum water. Give me the cup. I take it and look at a friend.
(Noh, p. 46)

The original

Waki: . . . <u>No matter how much he drinks, his face shows no change.</u> I thought it was so strange that <u>I asked his name.</u> He answered, "I am 'shojo', living in the sea." Today, I am waiting for that shojo at this bay of Shin'yo.
    Along the bay of Shin'yo, along the bay of Shin'yo,
I fill the jar with good sake of chrysanthemum;
And as if I were waiting for a friend who comes to admire the moon,
I wait, filling the cup with sake which reflects the moon.
Chorus: For staying young, for staying young, The name of the medicine is chrysanthemum water.
I will come to the surface of the water
Like the moon reflected on the sake cup.
It is indeed a pleasure to meet a friend,
To meet this friend. (Italics indicate the parts which agree with Pound's translation.)

In Pound's version, Waki's third sentence, "a shojo is a monkey," is inadequate, and three short sentences of the chorus hardly present the feeling of the original.

KUMASAKA

    The play is based on the story of the death of the great thief, Kumasaka Chohan (died 1174), at the hand of Ushiwakamaru (sometimes called Ushiwaka; later became Minamoto no Yoshitsune; 1159-1189), still a young boy. Kumasaka (in the form of a priest) asks the Waki (a travelling priest) to pray for a certain person, for this is the anniversary of that person's death. Kumasaka then invites the priest to stay overnight at his hut. The priest is surprised not to find the pictures and images of Buddha at Kumasaka's cottage; instead, the priest sees there a sword and other weapons unfit for a priest. Kumasaka then explains why he keeps the weapons--he uses them in order to protect the people from the robbers and thieves in the streets. When Kumasaka retires, the hut disappears and the priest finds himself in the grassy field under a pine-tree. Kumasaka reappears, revealing himself as Kumasaka Chohan, the famous thief. At the priest's request, Kumasaka tells the story of his last day: Kumasaka and his banditti waylaid Kichiji the gold-merchant, who was carrying a considerable amount of money. Kumasaka's banditti attack Kichiji and his attendants, but are soundly defeated by a young boy called Ushiwaka. Kumasaka decides on vengeance and challenges Ushiwaka. The two fight, and Kumasaka falls and dies. At the end of the story, Kumasaka disappears, wishing to attain Buddhahood, and the play ends.

The subject matter of the play is Kumasaka himself, or his changing attitudes before and after his death. While he was in flesh, he was a great thief; after his death, his ghost, in the form of a priest, protects the people from robbers. At his fight with the young Ushiwaka, Kumasaka was furious and angry, defeated by the youth; but, Kumasaka's ghost, returning to the world, praises the bravery of Ushiwaka. Also, the fact that the principal character is the wandering soul of Kumasaka in disguise, seeking to attain Buddhahood, shows that a religious element is important in this play. Pound, however, does not seem to realize this point and interprets the play mainly as a heroic tale of Kumasaka, whose bravery Pound holds in high esteem as if Kumasaka were not a thief but a warrior. Pound's remarks indicate that he slights the religious significance of the play: "Kumasaka [sic] is martial despite the touch of Buddhism in the opening scene, where the spirit is atoning for his past violence" (Noh, p. 54). Further, in translating the play, Pound leaves out two passages which are essential to the character of Kumasaka and to the subject matter of the play. First, in Kumasaka's seventh speech, Pound deletes the following lines:

> When I hear them [maids and servants] scream for help, I go out with this spear. And once in a while, I can prevent people from being robbed. Then I feel gratified to think that I am depended on by the people of this place. A feeling like this may be rather unbecoming for a priest who renounced the world.

The passage shows the changing attitudes of Kumasaka before and after his death--a change which is the subject matter of the play.

The second omission is in the final chorus of the play. In the original, the chorus describes how the ghost of Kumasaka disappears at the end of his story, leaving his last request: "Oh, help me to attain salvation." Pound's version does not include this last wish by Kumasaka. Since the primary objective of Kumasaka is to have the priest pray for his soul, it is important to present and to recapitulate Kumasaka's wish for salvation of his soul at the end of the play as the original does.

KAGEKIYO

The story of the play is as follows. Hitomaru (Tsure) has come to Hyuga in search of her father, Kagekiyo, who is said to be alive in exile in Hyuga. Hitomaru and her attendant come to a cottage in which lives an old blind beggar. They ask him if he knows an exile called Kagekiyo. The blind man says, "No." In reality, this old man is Kagekiyo himself, but he is too ashamed of his present condition to reveal his identity. Hitomaru and her attendant then meet a villager and ask him where Kagekiyo is. The villager tells them that they have met Kagekiyo without knowing him. The villager ushers Hitomaru and her attendant back to Kagekiyo. Without Kagekiyo's consent, the villager reveals his identity to the two visitors. Kagekiyo at first is distressed and even angry because he is thus known to them against his will. Soon, however, he is moved by his daughter's devotion which brought her to him. At her request, Kagekiyo tells a story of the battle which was won by his bravery. At the end of the story, Kagekiyo bids his daughter go home and she obeys. The play ends with the parting of the blind father and the young daughter. The subject matter is Kagekiyo himself: the play contrasts the misery and shame in which Kagekiyo lives as an old blind man with the bravery and confidence with which he fought in his youth as a warrior.

In Pound's translation of <u>Kagekiyo</u>, which has several incomplete and inadequate passages where the poet condenses the original at the sacrifice of its detailed descriptions or elaborate expressions, there is an example of an excellent handling of the original--the first two lines of the third speech of Kagekiyo: "Neither in the world of passion, nor in the world of colour, nor in the world of non-colour, is there any such place of rest" (<u>Noh</u>, p. 106). In these two lines Pound does not translate the original literally but paraphrases it, and the result is a distinct improvement, for a literal translation would not make the passage as clear or intelligible as Pound's translation does.

KAKITSUBATA

The story of the play is as follows: the Waki (a travelling priest) has come to Mikawa, where the iris are in full bloom. While he is watching the beautiful flowers, a woman comes and speaks to him. The priest asks her the name of the place. She says that it is called Yatsuhashi, famous for the iris ("kakitsubata"). And she quotes an iris poem attributed to Ariwara no Narihira[8] in <u>Ise Monogatari</u>.[9] She then invites the priest to stay overnight at her place. There she puts on a beautiful crown and a Chinese gown to show them to the priest. He asks what they signify. She explains that the Chinese gown is the one mentioned in Narihira's poem and the crown is what Narihira used to wear. The priest asks who she is. She says that she is the spirit of the iris, and that, since Narihira is the incarnation of the Bosatsu of music and dance in the Buddhist Paradise,[10] she, though not human, was able to attain Buddhahood, through his poem. She tells a little more about <u>Ise Monogatari,</u> dances a dance and disappears. And the play ends.

In this play the principal character (Shite) is the personification of the iris. The theme is a Buddhist belief that an iris which is not human can also attain Buddhahood by some proper help, here the special power given to Narihira, who in this play is glorified and considered as a Bosatsu of music and dancing.

In the opening part of <u>Kakitsubata</u>, the original text describes the simple fact of the passing spring and the approaching summer in ornate phrasing. A literal translation of the original would read something like this:

> Indeed time does not stop.
> Spring passes and summer is coming.
> Though it is said that the grass and trees do not have mind,
> The flowers do not forget their time.
> These may be called the flowers with beautiful appearance.
> Truly beautiful are these iris!

Pound's translation of the passage satisfactorily presents both the matter and the feeling of the original. Pound's version reads:

> Time does not stop and spring passes,
> The lightfoot summer comes nigh us,
> The branching trees and the bright unmindful grass
> Do not forget their time,
> They take no thought, yet remember
> To show forth their colour in season.
>   (Noh, pp. 122-123)

The ornamented language in which the original passage is written is lost in the literal translation given above. On the other hand, Pound, in my opinion, by expanding the original to some extent, succeeds in reproducing the fine tone of the original text. Particularly admirable is his handling of the paradoxical statements about the trees and grass which are "unmindful" and "take no thought" and yet "do not forget their time" and "remember/ To show forth their colour in season."

The play ends with the chorus telling how the heroine of the play, Kakitsubata, the spirit of the iris flower, is received to Buddhahood, employing a few images impressively and effectively. Pound successfully translates the original as follows:

> The sleeves are white like the snow of the Uno Flower
> Dropping their petals in April.
> Day comes, the purple flower
>   Opens its heart of wisdom,
> It fades out of sight by its thought.
> The flower soul melts into Buddha. (Noh, p. 130)

Pound's version reproduces with masterly assurance the seriousness of the subject--attainment of Buddhahood-- and the picturesqueness of the expression and the scene--the vivid images of "the snow of the Uno

Flower/Dropping their petals in April" and "the purple flower"--of the original.

HAGOROMO

The story is simple. Fisherman Hakuryo finds a feather-mantle ("hagoromo") hanging on a pine-tree and decides to keep it as treasure. Then an angel comes and begs him to return it to her, because without it she is unable to go back to heaven. At first Hakuryo refuses and the angel is greatly distressed. Finally Hakuryo begins to feel pity on her and offers to give back the feather-mantle if she promises to dance for him. The angel gladly promises to dance and asks for the mantle. Hakuryo says in reply that he will not hand it to her until she has danced, for, he says, if she has the mantle, she will leave without fulfilling her promise. Then the angel replies that lies are mortal and that angels do not deceive. Deeply ashamed of himself, Hakuryo gives back the mantle to her. The angel dances and finally disappears into the air and the play ends.

In this play the dance of the angel is important. In fact, the last half of the play is made up of the chants sung to the dancing. There is a clear contrast in the angel's emotions: in the first part, her grief over the loss of her feather-mantle dominates; in the second half, her joy over the recovery of it fills the play. The purity and innocence of the angel, a dweller of heaven, are contrasted with the human characteristics of selfishness, mercilessness, and suspicion shown in Hakuryo's reaction to the angel.

Toward the end of Hagoromo, the seventh chorus describes (in verse with irregular rhythmical patterns) the surrounding landscape in elaborate language. Pound translates the whole passage into prose. But, aside from this formal change and with the exception of one sentence in the middle which Pound misinterprets--instead of Pound's "O, you in the form of a maid, grant us the favour of your delaying," the original reads: "O, the wind, grant me a little more time to tarry here"--Pound's version presents the spirit of the original with a remarkable skill. It is a thorough, accurate translation with some parts appropriately paraphrased, especially those places where the original uses puns or some other rhetorical devices which are difficult to translate literally into meaningful English. Let us quote the entire passage:

> The spring mist is widespread abroad; so perhaps the wild olive's flower will blossom in the infinitely unreachable moon. Her flowery head-ornament is putting on colour; this truly is sign of the spring. Not sky is here, but the beauty; and even here comes the heavenly, wonderful wind. O blow shut the accustomed path of the clouds. O, you in the form of a maid, grant us the favour of your delaying. The pine-waste of Miwo puts on the colour of spring. The bay of Kiyomi lies clear before the snow upon Fuji. Are not all these presages of the spring? There are but few ripples beneath the piny wind. It is quiet along the shore. There is naught but a fence of jewels between the earth and the sky, and the gods within and without, beyond and beneath the stars, and the moon unclouded by her lord, and we who are born of the sun. This alone intervenes, here where the moon is unshadowed, here in Nippon, the sun's field. (Noh, p. 103)

CHORYO

The play is about Choryo (died 189 B.C.), a great vassal and military-strategist of Han dynasty, and Kosekko, a hermit-sage, known as the one who taught Choryo the strategy which enabled him to conquer neighboring enemies. The setting is in China. Waki (Choryo) had a dream in which he met, on an earthen bridge in Kahi, an old man on horseback, who dropped one of his shoes. Out of respect for the old man, Choryo picked it up for him. The old man then promised that he would teach Choryo art of warfare five days later on the same spot. On the promised day, when Choryo comes to the bridge, the old man is already there and scolds him for being late. The old man promises to teach him five days hence, and disappears. On the appointed day, this time, Choryo goes to the bridge before dawn. The old man, who is actually Kosekko, comes on horseback. Though he is quite sure of the worthiness and good nature of Choryo, he decides to try Choryo once more. Thus, Kosekko drops his shoe in the river. Immediately Choryo jumps into the river to recover the shoe, but the current is too fast. Then a huge snake appears in the river and snatches the shoe away. Choryo draws his sword and begins to attack the snake, which, apparently fearing the sword, returns the shoe to Choryo. Thus, recovering the shoe, Choryo comes out of the river, and helps Kosekko put it on. Satisfied with Choryo's spirits, Kosekko gives him a manual of military strategy. He also tells Choryo that the big snake was really Kannon (the Buddhist goddess of mercy) in disguise, who tried Choryo, and that Kannon will be Choryo's patron goddess from now on. The big snake then ascends to heaven and Kosekko climbs up a high mountain and turns into a yellow stone ("Kosekko" also means a yellow stone lord). The play ends here.

Pound's translation of Choryo is for the most part adequate, with only a phrasal omission (which is hardly significant) in Part II. Otherwise, there is no striking or serious problem. In fact, Choryo's first speech and the first chorus (both of Part II) are excellent translations of the original verse. Let us quote the two passages:

Choryo:
'Frost tinges the jasper terrace,
A fine stork, a black stork sings in the heaven,
Autumn is deep in the valley of Hako,
The sad monkeys cry out in the midnight,
The mountain pathway is lonely.'

Chorus:
The morning moonlight lies over the world
And flows through the gap of these mountains,
White frost is on Kahi bridge, the crisp water wrinkles beneath it,
There is no print in the frost on the bridge,
No one has been by this morning.
Chorio [Choryo], that is your luck. That shadow shows a man urging his horse.
(Noh, p. 132)

CONCLUSION

From the foregoing study of the fifteen plays translated by Pound, we may now summarize the quality, characteristics and problems which Pound's translations present. The study shows that the quality of Pound's translations of the plays is uneven, and that the kinds of problems they have vary from play to play. It is possible, however, to enumerate the most common characteristics of Pound's translations which are found in several, if not in all, plays: heavy cuts; omission of religious references; inadequate handling of parts with Buddhist pertinence; incomplete characterization; tendency toward condensation, simplification and prosaic translation; disregard of some of the typical Noh techniques; failure to understand situations; lack of knowledge of literary sources, resulting in incorrect translations; misunderstanding or misinterpretation of themes; minor phrasal inaccuracies; translations which are not literally faithful to the original but often more poetic than the original; tendency toward amplification and paraphrasing; and great craftsmanship in certain passages.

The fact that several characteristics are contradictory suggests that the result of Pound's translations was greatly pre-determined by the conditions of the Fenollosa manuscripts at the time they were handed to Pound. Without linguistic qualifications, Pound could not go to the original even when he found Fenollosa's draft incomplete or unintelligible. He had no choice but to present whatever he absorbed from Fenollosa's notes, often having to depend on his intuition, which sometimes misled him. Pound lacked the proper knowledge of Noh and of other cultural information to make significant changes in Fenollosa's notes. Nor does he seem to have checked with competent Japanese scholars.

It seems that the Fenollosa manuscripts were particularly poor in quality--incomplete and fragmentary--in the case of three plays: <u>Sotoba Komachi</u>, <u>Tamura</u> and <u>Tsunemasa</u>, and that Pound could not do much to improve the materials in front of him.[11] Consequently, Pound's translations of these plays contain many of the defects mentioned above. They suffer considerable cuts, have several passages greatly condensed at the sacrifice of both linguistic and stylistic charms of the original (detailed descriptions, intricate metaphors and elaborate expressions), and have some sections omitted, either entirely or in part, which are important to their subject matters or to the characterization of their principal figures. In each of these plays, Pound's translation leaves out a great part of the Buddhist references. Thus, Pound's translations lose the spirit and one essential aspect of the original, and it is usually the plot alone that Pound presents sufficiently. Also, because of the nature of the changes Pound makes--condensation and simplification--Pound's version of each of these plays tends to be more prosaic than the original.[12]

Pound's translations of another three plays--Kayoi Komachi, Aoi no Ue and Kumasaka--are more complete and have fewer omissions than the first three. However, in this second group of plays, again, Pound is inadequate in handling their religious elements. In some cases, Pound simply deletes the passages which have reference to Buddhism or Buddhist principles. In other cases, Pound presents an imperfect, or sometimes incomplete, rendering of the original, mainly because of his apparent lack of knowledge and understanding of the religious significance of the plays. In the case of Kumasaka, Pound slights the religious importance even though it is central to the play and emphasizes rather inappropriately the heroic aspect of the life of Kumasaka.

Aoi no Ue and Suma Genji have similarities. Both are based on the Tale of Genji, and both have some portions inadequately represented, probably because Pound was not sufficiently acquainted with the source, though the seriousness of misrepresentations differs in the two. Pound's misconception and misunderstanding of Aoi no Ue are fatal, whereas in Suma Genji Pound's misinterpretation is limited to only a part of the play.

The next four plays--Shojo, Genjo, Choryo, and Hagoromo--represent fairly good translations. Their problems are few and relatively minor, and in some sections, we find examples of successful rendering.

Finally, in the remaining three plays--Nishikigi, Kakitsubata and Kinuta--Pound presents an admirable translation of the original, successfully reproducing both the manner and the matter, and the form and the spirit of the original. In his translations of these plays Pound retains the formal and stylistic characteristics of the original to the highest degree. Here, in great contrast to such plays as Sotoba Komachi, Tamura, Tsunemasa and Kayoi Komachi, Pound's translation is thorough and complete, and often more poetic than the original. Sometimes, due to amplification, paraphrasing or addition, Pound's version cannot be considered faithful to the letter of the original, and yet it does present the sense, atmosphere and feelings of the original plays, and capture the tone of Noh.

Thus, it is in these three plays that we should look for the highest achievement of Pound's work on Noh. In these plays, Pound is successful not only in the translation but in the appreciation and understanding of the nature of Noh.

Of these three, <u>Kakitsubata</u> and <u>Kinuta</u> are slightly inferior to <u>Nishikigi</u>. <u>Kakitsubata</u> shows Pound's imperfect knowledge of the literary material on which the play is based, although this deficiency does not seriously affect the entire play. <u>Kinuta</u> has such weaknesses as the inadequate handling of religious references and a faulty ending. Everything considered, then, <u>Nishikigi</u>--though not flawless--is the best of Pound's translation of fifteen Noh plays, and interestingly enough, the first play to be published among the Fenollosa manuscripts.

Pound was a very great translator and student of non-Western cultures. At the same time he was a quick study and often presented himself as mastering civilizations of which he had, at best, an imperfect knowledge. Simultaneously he tended to be impatient with ascetic or religious-ascetic cultures, whether Christian or Buddhist, as his writing on those cultures in other contexts illustrates. One of the important tasks which remain to be accomplished in Pound scholarship is the examination of the extent to which his translations recreate the religious nuances and feel of the culture from which his originals came and the extent to which they merely use the culture's products to reinforce ideas and aesthetic modes of which Pound already approved. The same task remains to be done for the <u>Cantos</u> handling of non-Western and ancient Western cultures. In the case of the Japanese culture of the Noh play, Pound already had committed himself to Imagism and found in the Noh a reflection of his aesthetic ideas. In any case, he appears to have translated to suit his aesthetic and value predilections; but in the case of <u>Kakitsubata, Kinuta,</u> and <u>Nishikigi</u> he does more than that. He makes a translation which glorifies an art and philosophy not his own. That is, in itself, great art.

Notes to Chapter III

1. In Pound's version, "Itchiharano," "Ichihara" and "Ichihara-no-be" are errors for "Ichiwarano."

2. In the original, "my" of "my name" (pronounced "ono") and her name "Ono" make a pun. In other words, Ono gives her name indirectly by twice using the word "my" which contains the two syllables "ono," although she refuses to tell her name openly. Of course, it is extremely difficult to translate a pun in Japanese into English, and, moreover, it is doubtful that Pound knew of the pun here.

3. Pound's version omits two more parts which have religious pertinence: first, after the appearance of Shosho, the chorus (deleted by Pound) asks Shosho to accept the prayer together with Ono; and, second, after the identity of Shosho is known, the priest says: "Be persuaded to redeem your sin by repentance." (Pound leaves out this sentence in his translation of the priest's speech.)

4. In the Fenollosa manuscripts at Beinecke Library, there are five typed pages of the translation of Kayoi Komachi. The sentence in question here is not found in these five pages.

5. For example, Pound faithfully and fairly accurately presents a series of one-line speeches exchanged among Ono, Shosho and the chorus--the part describing Shosho's coming to Ono every night for ninety-nine days.

6. Chujo, sho sammi, naidaijin, dajodaijin, and dajotenno are the names of offices of the court in an ascending order of importance.

7. Part II appears in the last two pages of the translation of Genjo (12 handwritten pages) in the Fenollosa manuscripts at Beinecke Library, where the division into three speakers is observed.

8. A famous poet of noble birth; known for his handsome person and numerous love affairs (825-880). The central character of Ise Monogatari.

9. Ise Monogatari is the oldest utamonogatari (a poetic tale, or a tale consisting of many waka--a Japanese verse form of thirty-one syllables) in

Japanese literature. Love is the main theme. Neither the author nor the exact date is known (c. 950?).

10. Bosatsu or Bodhisattva. Here it means the highest-ranking deity of music and dance in the Buddhist Paradise called Gokuraku. The idea seemed to be popular at one time (probably in the ninth century) as a folk-legend in Japan.

11. Pound makes a notation that Fenollosa's translation of <u>Tamura</u> is fragmentary. See above.

12. Particularly in <u>Tamura</u>, Pound changes over sixty percent of the original verse to prose.

APPENDIX I

The following chart shows the proportion of verse and prose of Pound's translation in reference to corresponding portions in the original. I counted (1) the total number of lines of a play in Pound's translation; also under (1) is given what percentage Pound's version presents of the original text--in terms of the length. Pound's translations of Nishikigi and Kinuta are longer than the original due to additions. (2) the number of lines of the parts in Pound's translation which correspond to those in the original in terms of the style--whether prose or verse. (3) the number of lines in which Pound translates the original text written in prose into verse. (4) the number of lines in which Pound translates the original text written in verse into prose. And (5) the number of one-line speeches in Pound's translation in which it is impossible to determine (in English) whether they are prose or verse, although in the original it is possible to tell the style in which they are written. And then I give the percentage of each of items (2), (3), (4) and (5) in proportion to the total number of lines (1). In looking at the chart, however, we should not take the figures too strictly, but as an indication of the proportion of each item to the whole of a play. As we have seen, in some plays Pound adds words, phrases or lines to the original, while in some other plays Pound's translation presents only a part of the original text.

The fifteen plays are arranged according to the degree of the correspondence of the style (prose or verse) in Pound's translation to that of the original. Nishikigi has the greatest degree of the correspondence to the original in terms of the style. In all of the fifteen plays, except for Nishikigi, the proportion of item (4) is much greater than that of (3). That is, when Pound changes the style of the original in his translation, he almost always changes the original verse into prose. It is interesting to note that Kumasaka, which has the least correspondence to the original in regard to the style, has the highest proportion of the change of the original style--the change of the original verse into prose in Pound's translation--among the fifteen plays. Next to Kumasaka in the proportion of new prose are Tamura, Hagoromo, Tsunemasa and Genjo in descending order. Lastly, only in six plays does

95

Pound change the original prose into verse in his translation.

Title of the Play	(1)	(2)	(3)	(4)	(5)
Nishikigi	316 132%	262 83%	26 8%	22 7%	6 2%
Kakitsubata	181 97%	124 69%	13 7%	27 15%	17 9%
Kinuta	209 113%	131 63%	0	66 31%	12 6%
Sotoba Komachi	46 20%	27 59%	2 4%	17 37%	0
Suma Genji	95 68%	54 57%	14 15%	25 26%	2 2%
Choryo	70 94%	31 44%	0	30 43%	9 13%
Kagekiyo	154 58%	65 42%	3 2%	62 40%	24 16%
Aoi no Ue	112 68%	45 40%	0	45 40%	22 20%
Shojo	40 89%	14 35%	0	14 35%	12 30%
Tamura	72 64%	22 31%	0	46 64%	4 5%
Hagoromo	152 75%	42 28%	4 2%	95 63%	11 7%
Kayoi Komachi	79 65%	17 21%	0	33 42%	29 37%
Genjo	120 94%	19 16%	0	67 56%	34 28%
Tsunemasa	57 38%	8 14%	0	35 61%	14 25%
Kumasaka	124 65%	14 11%	0	80 65%	30 24%

APPENDIX II

TWO VERSIONS OF <u>YORO</u>

Ezra Pound's "translation" of a Japanese Noh play, <u>Yoro</u> (not included in <u>Noh</u>), was published in <u>Paideuma</u>, Volume 4, Numbers 2 & 3. The text of the Pound version and my translation of the original play with some notes on the Pound text are given here. (My translation was originally published in <u>Paideuma</u>, Volume 10, Number 2.)

THE POUND VERSION

YORO

(name of the waterfall in Mino)

by Motokiyō

1st SHITE   a father
TSURE   his son
WAKI   an imperial messenger
2ND SHITE   God of Mt. Temple

Scene in Mino

WAKI: (<u>sings</u>) Winds are calm--All the leaves & branches are quiet. (reign is prosperous) (Kotoba) I am a subject to the Emperor Yuriaku. Some one told him that a wonderful fountain is in this province of Motosu in Mino. So I received his order to see it quickly. So I am now making haste to Motosu.
(Michiyuki) It is peaceful--the land is wealthy, and the people are rich. There are roads everywhere. The gates of the passes are opened. Passing the way of Mino which I heard far in the country I came to the fall of Yoro.

SHITE & TSURE: How the water is clear! Under the shade of the pines! in the mountain of Mino! which pines have passed so many years!

TSURE: The hill of age who is familiar to me--

TOGETHER: How quiet are our hearts to pass!

SHITE: My old friends were already awakened from their dream of the world (or dead). and I passed the flower time of less and more.

SHITE & TSURE: My heart longs for the moon of a thatched house; and my body floats like the frost on a wooden bridge. Though the clouds of white head gather now, the water of the fall which consoles age will make clear my heart. (Yōrō = yō = feeding & consoling--rō = age)
(Sing) Is this the custom in the deep valley of far off mountains? However I dip the water, it is not extinguished. In the house of Chosei (long living) is the gate which will not become old (this refers to the gates of some Chinese temple Choseiden, and Furōmon).
But here, living in this mountain, under the shade of a pine tree, and using the water of the fountain as medicine, and prolonging our age, how hopeful are we, how happy our prospects!

WAKI: I have something to ask of the old man there.

SHITE: You mean me? What's the matter?

WAKI: Are you the father & the son of whom I heard so much?

SHITE: Yes. We are a father & a son.

WAKI: I am the imperial messenger.

SHITE: O how thankful! To receive the words of the Emperor whom I see far up in the sky with this wretched body, how thankful it is! We are father and son.

WAKI: Someone told the Emperor that a wonderful fountain pours from Motosu. He ordered me to go quickly and see it. So tell me in detail why it is called Yōrō.

SHITE: Yes. This is my son. In the morning in the evening, he goes to the mountain, and takes fuel, and feeds me. Once, being weary of mt. road, he dipped this water in his hand and drank it, but strangely his heart was quite refreshed, and he recovered.

TSURE: Thinking the medicine water of the house of Sennin will be such, I went home dipping the water and carrying it, and gave to the father and mother.

SHITE: We drank it, and unconsciously we forgot our age.

TSURE: From that it was not difficult to get up so early in the morning.

TOGETHER: It was not so solitary even when we were awakened from dreams in the night. Some vigor and courage came to us: and as this true clear water consoles our age unceasingly, it is called the Fall of Yōrō

WAKI: Indeed! How grateful! I think there is some special place in this river where the water of medicine pours out.

SHITE: Look. It is the fountain of water from the rock. A little on this side from the basin below.

WAKI: Then is this the fountain. So saying he approached and looked at it. He found it was very clear.

SHITE: The small pebbles becoming rocks having covering of moss.

WAKI: The happy example which continues to a thousand generations.

SHITE: I see here in this medicine of waters

WAKI: Truly this!

SHITE: Consoles the age.

CHORUS: If it consoles (invigorates) age, then it will be the best medicine to the people of ripe age, And their lives will not end, forever. O how happy is this fountain! Indeed, as this of the reign which is clear on the upper Emperor part of the gem (source) water, so even we who are in the very end (mouth) of the stream (people) can live happily.

CHORUS: (Kuru) Indeed as the island of Yomogi (Horai) is very far in this age, though we search it, how can we find such example? The medicine of Life, water upon water, it is quite inexhaustible.

SHITE: Though the course of water which flows is not extinguished, but it is not the water of the old! (famous quotation from Kamo no Chomei's Hōjōki)

CHORUS: The bubbles which float on this stream they disappear and they come again. O how clear is this colour.

SHITE: Specially this is of the moment of summer. unparalleled.

CHORUS: And who found this happy sign, to make water as medicine? We will dip the water! We will dip the water! The bamboo leaves of a jar will glow in shade (ehikuyo = sake). The Tekika (flowers of ashi = reed) beside the hedge dips the autumn of the forest leaves. (obscure in origin) The pleasure of 7 sages of Shin as the play of Ryunhakurin (he was one of the 7 sages, who made a famous essay on plays of sake) all are in this water, O dip! O dip! This medicine. I will offer to you the cup floating on the winding water (kiokusin = narrow stream (palace garden)) (on the feast called Kiokusin en) will strike against a rock and will be very slow (to drink)! So I will dip it with my hands, and through the whole night I will dip the moon.

CHORUS: (Rongi) Who was invigorated? By the water & the deep mountain.

SHITE: We hear that it was by virtue of water that Hoso by the vigor of dew of the chrysanthemum lived for 700 years.

CHORUS: Indeed, while I dipped the water of kiku in that very short space, (hearing it was a medicine) (kiku = hear Tsuyu no ma = little space) (double play of double meaning)

SHITE: We passed a thousand years.

CHORUS: Heaven & Earth opened, and even the grass & plants--

SHITE: blossomed and bore fruit.

CHORUS: Season after season

SHITE: Only by the blessing of rain and dew.

CHORUS: By nursing the old man which is like the dew and rain, the parents of flowers were invigorated. And I became familiar to this water. My sleeves were torn, and the shadow of my hands dipping the water is clearly seen in this mountain well. As to think this a medicine, so my figure of old age seems to me as young water. O how happy!

WAKI: O how wonderful, this water! I will go back to my lord quickly and tell him.

SHITE: (That young water is the water of the New Year) The old man felt very grateful for these blessings.

WAKI: The imperial messenger fell in tears. How wonderful that I met such a thing! (sings) As he did not finish this saying-- strange! a light gleaming from heaven, the thunder of falls became quiet, music was heard, and flowers rained. It was not thought a common thing.

2ND SHITE: O how grateful! As the custom of the peaceful reign the mountains, the river, the grass, and the peasants are calm. Winds on every 5th day and rain on every 10th day. The shining sun is lovely in the sky and the fountain of medicine of that green water will not fail. O how grateful are men!

CHORUS: Even I who guard this reign, where the water is inextinguishable--

SHITE: I am the God of the Temple of this mountain (Kami & Buddha are the same)

CHORUS: Or you may call me Yorin (willow) Kuanon Bosatsu

SHITE: The God Kami

CHORUS: The Buddha Hotoke.

SHITE: These are only separation of names.

CHORUS: And are the voice of means to save the people.

SHITE: The storm of the mt., the water of the valley.

CHORUS: The sound goes in harmony. The sound of music makes clear the heart of the falls. O the Shadow of many heavens!

SHITE: The green of the pine tree seems to have passed 1000 years.

CHORUS: The clear clear well of the mt.

SHITE: The water flows & flows, and the waves are calm. The lord of the peaceful reign is the ship—

CHORUS: The lord is the ship, the subject is the water. The water will make the ship float. The subject looks up and reverences the lord. Such a reign will be eternal. Led by the lord of gem water the subject on the lower part becomes clear too. O a good reign! O a good reign! I will repeat this, as the waves on the full basin come back.

THE ORIGINAL TEXT

Yōrō[1]
by Zeami Motokiyo

Shite (First Shite): an old man of the village; a father
Tsure: his son
Waki: an imperial messenger
Waki Tsure: an official accompanying him
Second Shite: the god of the mountain temple at the waterfall of Yōrō

Waki & Waki Tsure: The wind is calm; the wind is calm;
The oak leaves make no sound,
And their branches are at rest.
All is peaceful.

Waki: I am a subject of the Emperor Yūryaku. It is reported to the Throne that a wonderful fountain has gushed out in the county of Motosu, in the province of Mino. At His Majesty's imperial command to make haste and examine it, I am now hurrying to the county of Motosu in Mino Province.

Waki & Waki Tsure: A peaceful reign!
The land is rich,
The people well-off.
The land is rich,
The people well-off.
The roads lead in all directions;
The gates[2] are open throughout the nation.
In the far off country is Mino
Whose name is heard [in the city].
Yet in a short time
I traveled the roadway to Mino.
I have arrived at the Falls of Yōrō.
I have arrived at the Falls of Yōrō.

Shite & Tsure: In the mountain of Mino,
I have lived for many years
Under the shadow of the age-old pine trees.
How clear the water is,
Reflecting their green color!

Tsure: This hill is familiar
To the old man that I am;

Shite & Tsure: It is easy to climb
With my heart carefree.

Shite: Old men awake early from their sleep;
Their dreams are but the flowers of the past,
Sixty years gone by.

Shite & Tsure: My heart chants poems for the moon over the thatched roof;
My body roams about the frost on the wooden bridge.

Though the snow piles on my white hair,
The water of the falls which nurtures old age cleanses my heart.
Like the famous water in the deep valley of far-off mountains[3],
The water [of this fall] will never be exhausted,
However much one takes from it.
The water [of this fall] will never be exhausted,
However much one takes from it.
In the imperial palace, Chōsei-den[4],
In the imperial palace, Chōsei-den,
The ageless gate is said to stand.
Though I am an old man living in the mountain,
I look forward to a life long as that of a pine tree.
Under its shade, the water coming out of the rocks is the medicine
The medicine that delays aging.
In my heart I feel I still have a long future.
In my heart I feel I still have a long future.

Waki: Listen, the old man there!

Shite: Are you calling me? What is it you desire?

Waki: Are you the father and the son of whom I heard so much?

Shite: Yes, we are a father and a son.

Waki: I am the imperial messenger.

Shite: How auspicious! What a rare blessing for a humble man to receive the edict of His Majesty, who reigns at the imperial palace which is far away from here. Yes, we are the father and the son.

Waki: It is reported to the Throne that a wonderful fountain has appeared in the county of Motosu. Following the imperial command to hurry and see it, I was sent to this place as the imperial messenger. First of all, tell me in detail the origin of the name Yōrō.

Shite: This man here is my son. Morning and evening he goes to the mountain, gathers firewood, and cares for us. One day, being tired on the mountain road, he casually dipped his hand in this water and drank. To his surprise, his heart was refreshed and his fatigue gone.

Tsure: Thinking that the medicinal water of the region of <u>sennin</u>[5] must be such, I took some, carried it on my way home, and gave it to my father and mother.

Shite: As soon as we drank it, we forgot our old age;

Tsure: No longer was it difficult to get up early in the morning;

Shite & Tsure: Nor was it lonesome to wake up in the night.
My spirits are high, and as this true clear water consoles my old age unceasingly, it is called the Falls of Yōrō.

Waki: Indeed! What a blessing I've heard! Is there some special place in this river where this medicinal water pours out, I wonder?

Shite: Please look. There is the fountain springing from the rock, a little on this side of the bottom of the fall.

Waki: So this is the fountain.
So saying, he approached and looked at it.
It is truly a pure mountain spring.

Shite: It is as though I were witnessing
Those pebbles at the clear bottom
Become rocks covered with moss,

Waki: As the happy sign of continuation
Through thousands upon thousands of years.

Shite: This medicinal water does,

Waki: truly, old age,

Shite: console.

Chorus: If it consoles old age,
Then it will be good medicine to the people in their prime.
[If the Emperor drinks this water,]
His Majesty's life will be endless.
What a blissful fountain!

Indeed, since this Emperor's reign is as clear and pure as this upstream water, even we, who are in the end of the stream, are happy, living a good life; we are happy, living a good life.

Chorus (Kuri)[6]:
Indeed, no matter how hard we may search,
The island of Yomogi[7] is not to be found.
Yet here is the real example of the medicine of life;
Water upon water, it is inexhaustible.

Shite: Though the flow of the river never ceases,
It is not the water of the old.

Chorus: The bubbles which float on this stream
Now disappear and now come again;
But the color of the water is always clear.

Shite: Especially this is unparalleled--

Chorus: The water which flows underneath the summer mountain has turned into medicine.--
Who has seen such a happy omen?

Chorus: We will take some water.
We will take some water.

Chorus: As bamboo leaves in the sun deepen their shade of green,
The *sake* in a jar is said to mellow in spring.
Also one drinks *sake* as the reed-flowers along the fence
Remind one of the autumn color of the forest leaves.
The pleasure of the seven sages of Shin,
The delight of Ryūhakurin,[8]
All remains in this water.
Let us drink! Let us drink!
Let us offer this medicine to His Majesty!

Chorus: The ōmu cup[9] floating on the winding stream
May be blocked by a rock and arrive slowly,
But let us take hold of the cup, and through the night,
Let us together take some of the moon[-reflecting water];
Let us together take some of the moon[-reflecting water].

Chorus: Who was nurtured by the water in the deep mountain?

Shite: Hōso, we hear, was nurtured by the dew drops from chrysanthemum, granted the virtue of <u>sennin,</u> and lived for seven hundred years -- all <u>owing</u> to the medicinal water.

Chorus: In truth, it is said, the chrysanthemum water is medicine; nurtured by its dews, in a brief time

Shite: One passes a thousand years.
Since the beginning of heaven and earth,

Chorus: Even the grass and trees

Shite: Blossom and bear fruit

Chorus: According to their seasons, it is said.

Shite: But it is by the blessing of rain and dew

Chorus: That they are nurtured.
Rain and dew are the parents of flowers.
An old man, I, too, am nourished by this familiar water.
I dip my hand in the water,
Wetting my sleeve.
And I see my hand reflected in this mountain spring.
As I truly believe this is medicine,
My figure of old age seems young.
How happy I am!

Waki: O how wonderful! this medicinal water!
I will return to His Majesty in a hurry and give a report.
How happy I am!

Shite: The old man showed his reverence for the munificent lord who gave this blessing.

Waki: The imperial messenger, too, fell in tears.
How wonderful that I encountered such a miracle!

Chorus: How strange! How strange!
Hardly had he finished these words,
Hardly had he finished these words,
When the light shone in the sky;
The sound of the falls became clear;

Music was heard and flowers rained.
It seemed no ordinary occurrence;
It seemed no ordinary occurrence.

Second Shite: How wonderful!
As the sign of the peaceful reign,
The mountains, the rivers, the grass, and the trees are calm.
Winds [blow] on every fifth day; rain [falls] on every tenth day.
The sun shines in the sky.
The cloudless, pure water of the medicinal fountain will never be exhausted.
It is an auspicious omen, indeed.

Chorus: This too is a divine pledge of the Law of Buddha, protecting the ever-lasting reign.

Second Shite: I am the god of this mountain temple,

Chorus: Also called Yōryū Kannon Bosatsu.[10]

Second Shite: Kami [the god],

Chorus: Or Hotoke [Buddha],

Second Shite: -- Their difference is in names only like the water and the waves.

Chorus: They show themselves to save the people.

Second Shite: The storm over the mountain and the water of the valley,

Chorus: These are harmonious sounds of music.
As we calm our stirring hearts by the side of the waterfall,
Heavenly gods make their appearance.

Second Shite: The green of the pine trees [mirrored in the water] seems to reflect a thousand years,

Chorus: So clear is the water of the mountain spring,
The water of the mountain spring.
In the mountain spring,

Second Shite: Swiftly does the water flow;
Calm are the waves
In the peaceful reign,
His Majesty is the ship,

His Majesty is the ship;
The subject is the water.
The water makes the ship float;
The subject looks up to His Majesty.
Such a reign will never cease, will never cease.
Led by His Majesty, the upper stream of the gem
water is clear,
And the lower stream becomes also limpid.
Like the bouyant waves of the waterfall,
Turning and turning,
This is a good reign;
This is a good reign.
With my blessing for ten thousand years,
With my blessing for ten thousand years,
I shall return [to heaven];
I shall return [to heaven].

Footnotes

1. "Yōrō" literally means "to console old age"; it is also the name of the waterfall in this play.

2. Major roads had barriers or checking stations to inspect travelers.

3. The legendary sacred water in China; anyone who drinks is said to enjoy a long life.

4. "Chōsei-den" means "a palace of long life."

5. "Sennin": A legendary hermit who acquired immortality through religious asceticism. (Cf. <u>Annotated Index to The Cantos of Ezra Pound</u>, p. 196 and <u>A Companion to the Cantos of Ezra Pound</u>, Vol. I, p. 14.)

6. "Kuri": a term designating a tone of chanting.

7. "Yomogi": also called "Hōrai-san"; a legendary land of eternal youth and immortality.

8. "Ryūhakurin": one of the seven sages of Shin.

9. "Ōmu cup": A beautiful cup made of a seashell.

10. "Yōryū Kannon Bosatsu": name of a Bodhisattva.

NOTES ON THE POUND VERSION

A comparison of the "Pound" version and the translation of the original reveals that the former is more like a working draft. In the Pound version, no apparent attempt is made to distinguish between prose and verse; and editorial comments and explanations are given in parentheses in the text. Also, repetitions which are frequent in the original are omitted. While the translation of the original should clarify most of ambiguities in the Pound version, a few additional notes which follow may be useful.

Waki's first speech:
    Kotoba: a term designating the spoken (as distinguished from sung) part.

    Yuriyaku: The emperor's name, Yūryaku, spelled incorrectly.

    Michiyuki: a term signifying a journey (i.e., Waki is traveling).

The first speech by Shite & Tsure together through Shite's first speech (from "which pines have passed so many years!" to "and I passed the flower time of less and more"):
    The Pound version is inaccurate and almost unintelligible. "My old friends were already awakened from their dreams of the world (or dead)" is a misinterpretation.

The third speech by Shite & Tsure together:
    The original has "snow" instead of "clouds" in "Though the clouds of white head. . ."

Waki's second speech through the first chorus:
    The Pound version is mostly satisfactory.

The second Chorus:
    Kuru: an error for "Kuri." See Footnote 6 of my translation.

The fourth Chorus (from "The bamboo leaves of a jar" to "autumn of the forest leaves"):
    The translation of this part is difficult because the playwright uses highly condensed and even

elliptical expressions, and at the same time, assumes the understanding of allusions used here.

The fifth Chorus:
Rongi: a term designating the part in which Shite and Chorus (and sometimes another character) alternate the chanting.

The ninth Chorus (from "By nursing the old man" to "My sleeves were torn"):
The Pound version has some inaccuracies. "My sleeves were torn" should read "My sleeve is wet."

Shite's 17th speech:
"(That young water is the water of the New Year.)" This editorial comment is unintelligible. The original has no corresponding passage.

Second Shite's first speech:
"the peasants" is not in the original.

The tenth Chorus:
"Even I who guard this reign" is not in the original.

Second Shite's second speech:
"(Kami & Buddha are the same.)" should not be here. This editorial note, however, could be an explanation for (Second) Shite's third speech through his fourth speech:

Shite: The God Kami
Chorus: The Buddha Hotoke
Shite: These are only separation of names.

The eleventh Chorus:
"Yorin" should be "Yōryū" and "Kuanon" should be "Kannon."

The final (16th) Chorus omits the last lines of the original text.

BIBLIOGRAPHY

(Works Cited in This Study)

I. Works by Ernest Fenollosa and Ezra Pound:

Fenellosa, Ernest F. <u>Epochs of Chinese and Japanese Art: An Outline History of East Asiatic Design</u>. New and revised edition, with copious notes by Professor Petrucci. New York: Dover Publications, Inc., 1963. 2 vols.

_____, and Pound, Ezra. <u>The Chinese Written Character as a Medium for Poetry</u>. [and] <u>Confucius. The Unwobbling Pivot & The Great Digest</u>. Translated by Ezra Pound. New York: Kasper & Horton Publishers. [no date].

_____. <u>The Classic Noh Theatre of Japan</u>. New York: New Directions, 1959. Sixth Printing.

Pound, Ezra. <u>ABC of Reading</u>. New York: New Directions, 1960.

_____. <u>The Cantos of Ezra Pound</u>. New York: New Directions, 1972.

_____. <u>Cathay</u>. Translations by Ezra Pound. London: Elkin Matthews, 1915.

_____. <u>EP to LU: Nine Letters Written to Louis Untermeyer by Ezra Pound</u>. Edited by J.A. Robbins. Bloomington, Indiana: Indiana University Press, 1963.

_____. <u>Guide to Kulchur</u>. New York: New Directions, 1952.

_____. <u>Make it New: Essays by Ezra Pound</u>. New Haven: Yale University Press, 1935.

_____. <u>Selected Letters of Ezra Pound 1907-1941</u>. Edited by D.D. Paige. New York: New Directions, 1971.

_____. "Yoro," <u>Paideuma</u>. (Fall-Winter 1975) Vol. 4, Nos. 2 & 3, pp. 349-353.

II. Other Works:

Edwards, John Hamilton, et al. Annotated Index to the Cantos of Ezra Pound. Cantos I - LXXXIV. Berkeley and Los Angeles: University of California Press, 1957.

Kenner, Hugh. Pound Era. Berkeley and Los Angeles: University of California Press, 1971.

Miner, Earl. The Japanese Tradition in British and American Literature. Princeton: Princeton University Press, 1958.

Nassar, Eugene Paul. The Cantos of Ezra Pound: The Lyric Mode. Baltimore and London: The Johns Hopkins University Press, 1975.

Norman, Charles. Ezra Pound. New York: The Macmillan Co., 1960.

Stock, Noel. ed. Ezra Pound. Perspectives. Essays in Honor of His Eightieth Birthday. Chicago: Henry Regnery Co., 1965.

_____. Poet in Exile. Ezra Pound. New York: Barnes & Noble, Inc., 1964.

Stopes, Marie C. Plays of Old Japan. The 'No'. New York, 1913.

Teele, Roy E. "A Balance Sheet on Pound's Translations of Noh Plays," Books Abroad. (Summer 1965) Vol. 39, pp. 168-170.

Terrell, Carroll E. A Companion to the Cantos of Ezra Pound. Berkeley, Los Angeles, London: University of California Press, 1980. Vol. 1 (Cantos 1-71).

Waley, Arthur. The No Plays of Japan. New York: Grove Press , Inc., 1957.

III. Works in Japanese:

Choryo. Edited by Kanze Sakon. Tokyo: Hinoki Shoten, 1966.

Furukawa, Hisashi. Noh no Sekai ["The World of Noh"]. Tokyo: Shakai Shiso sha, 1960.

Genjo. Edited by Kanze Sakon. Tokyo: Hinoki Shoten, 1966.

Kakitsubata. Edited by Kanze Sakon. Tokyo: Hinoki Shoten, 1966.

Nishikigi. Edited by Kanze Sakon. Tokyo: Hinoki Shoten, 1966.

Suma Genji. Edited by Kanze Sakon. Tokyo: Hinoki Shoten, 1965.

Tamura. Edited by Kanze Sakon. Tokyo: Hinoki Shoten, 1966.

Yokyoku Shu ["The Collection of Noh Plays"]. Edited by Mario Yokomichi and Akira Omote. Tokyo: Iwanami Shoten, 1960 (Vol. II).

INDEX

Since this book is a study of Ezra Pound's work in The Classic Noh Theatre of Japan (identified as Noh in the text), neither Pound nor Noh is indexed.

ABC of Reading (Pound), 28

Aoi no Ue (play title), ix, xi, 1, 3, 4, 6, 15, 21, 22, 29, 46-53, 54, 77, 90, 96

Aoi no Ue (character), 46, 47, 48, 49, 50, 51, 64

Ariga, Nagao, 12

Awoi no Ue, see Aoi no Ue

Buddhism, see Noh: religious elements

Buss, Kate, 26

Cantos (Pound), 14, 15, 16, 17, 18, 21, 22, 28, 66, 91

Cathay (Pound), 26, 28

The Chinese Written Character as a Medium for Poetry (Fenollosa and Pound), 28

Choryo (play title), 3, 4, 87-88, 90, 96

Fenollosa, Ernest, ix, x, xi, 7, 8, 9, 10, 11, 12, 14, 15, 22, 24, 25, 26, 28, 31, 34, 36, 37, 41, 46, 47, 48, 49, 55, 56, 63, 65, 69, 73, 89, 91, 92, 93

Fenollosa, Mary, 7, 8, 10, 11, 24, 25

Genji (character), 50, 52, 64, 77, 78

Genjo (play title), 3, 4, 10, 78-80, 90, 92, 95, 96

Guide to Kulchur (Pound), 14, 28, 29

Hagoromo (play title), ix, xi, 3, 4, 13, 15, 16, 17, 21, 65, 86-87, 90, 95, 96

Hajitomi (play title), 50

Hikaru Genji, see Genji

Hirata, Kiichi, 10, 31, 49

Hughes, Glenn, 11, 25

Ibsen, Henrik, 48

Ise Monogatari, 6, 24, 84, 92

Kagekiyo (play title), 3, 4, 15, 18, 19, 28, 83-84, 96

Kakitsubata (play title), 1, 3, 4, 6, 14, 46, 84-86, 90, 91, 96

Kan'ami, 1, 24, 34

Kayoi Komachi (play title), 3, 4, 15, 22, 29, 54, 58, 67-72, 90, 92, 96

Kenner, Hugh, 25

Kinuta (play title), ix, xi, 1, 3, 4, 54-61, 90, 91, 95, 96

Kitasono, Katue, 12

Kiyotsugu, see Kan'ami

Komachi, see Ono no Komachi

Kumasaka (play title), 3, 4, 15, 17, 18, 65, 81-83, 90, 95, 96

Lady Murasaki, 6, 20, 77

Lowell, Amy, 9

Make It New (Pound), 26

Miner, Earl, xi

Monroe, Harriet, 8, 9

Mori, Kainen, 12

Motokiyo, see Zeami

Murasaki, see Lady Murasaki

Naidu, Sarojini, 7

Nassar, Eugene Paul, 22, 30

<u>Nishikigi</u> (play title), ix, 1, 3, 4, 9, 14, 27, 40-45, 90, 91, 95, 96

Noh:

    description of form, ix, 1-6

    images and Imagisme, 13-14, 22

    literary style, 5-6, 74, 95-96

    religious elements, 33, 34-35, 39, 43-45, 50-53, 58-59, 62-63, 69-72, 72-74, 75-77, 82-83, 84-86, 92

<u>'Noh' or Accomplishment: A Study of the Classical Stage of Japan</u> (Fenollosa and Pound), 7, 10

Norman, Charles, 24

Ono no Komachi (character), 33, 34, 36, 37, 38, 39, 67, 68, 69, 70, 71, 92

Pound, Dorothy, 8

Quinn, John, 11, 28

Rokujo (character), 46, 47, 48, 49, 50, 51, 52, 53, 64

<u>Selected Letters of Ezra Pound 1907-1941</u>, 8, 9, 10, 11, 12, 25, 27, 28

Shii no Shosho (character), 33, 37, 38, 39, 67, 71, 92

Shite, 1, 46, 54, 73, 84, 97-108

<u>Shojo</u> (play title), 3, 4, 80-81, 90, 96

Shosho, <u>see</u> Shii no Shosho

<u>Sotoba Komachi</u> (play title), ix, xi, 3, 4, 15, 22, 29, 33-39, 54, 58, 67, 69, 72, 73, 89, 90, 96

Stock, Noel, 8, 25

<u>Suma Genji</u> (play title), 1, 3, 4, 6, 14, 15, 19, 21, 77-78, 90, 96

Takasago (play title), 13, 15

Tale of Genji, 6, 20, 46, 52, 77, 78, 90

Tamura (play title), ix, 3, 4, 72-74, 89, 90, 93, 95, 96

Teele, Roy E., xi, 10, 27, 31, 62

Terrell, Carroll F., 22, 29

Tsunemasa (play title), 3, 4, 75-77, 89, 90, 95, 96

Tsure, 1, 46, 54, 67, 97-108

Umewaka, Minoru, 7, 12, 31

Untermeyer, Louis, 8

Waki, 1, 46, 54, 67, 73, 75, 77, 80, 81, 87, 97-108

Waley, Arthur, xi, 6, 10, 24, 34, 47, 49, 51, 52, 62

Williams, William Carlos, 8

Yeats, W. B., 10

Yoro (play title), 97-111

Yugao (character), 50, 51, 52

Zeami, 1, 24, 97, 102